Test Prep

Grade 5

FlashKids

New York

© 2005 by Spark Publishing
Adapted from *Test Best for Test Prep, Level E*
© 1999 by Harcourt Achieve
Licensed under special arrangement with Harcourt Achieve.

For more information, please visit www.flashkids.com
Please submit all inquiries to Flashkids@sterlingpublishing.com

ISBN 978-1-4114-0401-4

Manufactured in China

Lot #:
28 30 29 27
11/20

Production by Creative Media Applications

TABLE OF CONTENTS

FOR TEST-SMART PARENTS

As you know, standardized tests are an important part of your child's school career. These tests are created by your state's education department and set to its standards of learning for each grade level. These tests are valuable tools that measure how much your child knows in the areas of reading and math. *Test Prep: Grade 5* is designed to familiarize your child with test formats and directions, teach test-taking strategies, and provide practice in skill areas that most states consider important. This workbook will also help your child review the basic skills taught in the fifth grade.

Preparation is the key to helping your child become test-smart. Practicing basic skills in a testing situation can help ensure that your child's scores reflect his or her understanding of the material presented in school. Test-smart students:

- are comfortable in the testing environment;

- know how to approach different kinds of test questions;

- apply knowledge to a variety of test formats;

- use time wisely during tests.

Completing the practice exercises and tests in this workbook can help your child relax and feel ready as test day approaches. This practice also provides a review of the essential skills that will help your child with coursework during the school year.

ABOUT THIS WORKBOOK

Test Prep: Grade 5 is divided into three helpful sections. Practice exercises and mini-tests introduce and review basic test-taking skills. Longer practice tests that mirror the actual tests your child will encounter at school appear at the end of the book.

- **Unit 1: Test-Taking Strategies**
  These pages help your child learn essential strategies to use during any standardized test. You might read these pages together with your child. Talk about which strategies your child has used before and which ones are new.

- **Units 2–7: Mini-Tests**
  Each unit focuses on a subject found on standardized tests: reading comprehension, reading vocabulary, mathematics, problem solving, and language. These mini-tests help your child learn specific test strategies. Each unit concludes with a unit test that covers all of the skills in the unit's lessons.

- **Units 8–11: Practice Tests**
  These longer practice tests help your child apply test-taking skills in a realistic testing environment. He or she will mark answers on the sheet at the back of this workbook. By familiarizing your child with the experience, these practice tests can lessen feelings of intimidation during school tests.

Throughout the mini-tests, hints and Test Tips will draw your child's attention to useful ways to approach individual problems. Test Tips do not appear in the final practice tests, which reflect realistic testing situations.

These tests help your child develop four important skills that are crucial in testing situations. Familiarize yourself with these goals in order to support your child's development of these skills.

USING TIME WISELY

All standardized tests are timed. Your child needs to understand how to manage time wisely. Review these strategies together:

- Work rapidly but comfortably.
- Do not spend too much time on any one question.
- Mark items to return to if there is enough time.
- Use any remaining time to review answers.
- Use a watch to keep track of time.

AVOIDING ERRORS

Your child can practice these strategies when choosing the correct answers on standardized tests:

- Pay careful attention to directions.
- Determine what is being asked.
- Mark answers in the appropriate place.
- Check all answers.
- Do not make stray marks on the answer sheet.

REASONING

Standardized tests require your child to think logically when answering each question. These strategies can help your child think through each question before choosing the best answer:

- Before answering a question, read the entire question or passage and all the answer choices.
- Restate questions and answer choices in your own words.
- Apply skills learned in class and practice situations.

GUESSING

Your child can learn the best thing to do when the correct answer is not clear right away. Suggest these hints as helpful solutions if a question seems difficult:

- Try to answer all of the questions within the allotted time. Do not spend too much time on a question that seems hard.
- Eliminate answers that you know are incorrect. If you cannot do this, skip the question.
- Compare the remaining answers. Restate the question, and then choose the answer that seems most correct.

Daily encouragement and support for learning will help your child feel confident and secure. Every student needs much experience with reading and exposure to a wide variety of reading material. The school curriculum is carefully designed to teach skills your child needs to become a proficient learner. Your home environment is another essential part of the education equation. Here are some ways you can help your child year-round.

CREATE A QUIET STUDY SPACE

A quiet, clean, and cheerful study space will help your child develop strong study habits. Provide a study area with an open workspace. Make sure that writing supplies like paper and pencils are nearby, as well as tools like a calculator, ruler, scissors, glue, and a dictionary. You might also create files or boxes to store your child's work. Make separate files for finished works and works in progress.

BE A HOMEWORK HELPER

Talk about homework assignments with your child. Your questions can help your child focus on what is important about the task or project. Your interest in schoolwork will encourage your child's enthusiasm and dedication. Check in while your child is working to see if you can answer any questions or help find solutions. Just letting your child know that you care can promote active learning.

USE THE INTERNET EFFECTIVELY

Many fifth graders use the Internet as a reference source. Monitor your child's use of the Internet, and together decide if a Web site probably contains information that is correct. Look for Internet sites sponsored by educational organizations (many of which have URLs that end with *.edu*). Remind your child that sites written by other students may not have been checked carefully for accuracy. Try to back up important information with library sources, such as encyclopedias and other books.

PRACTICE WITH A CALCULATOR

Many standardized tests allow students to use calculators. Make sure you have a calculator at home that is in good working condition. Calculators do not replace the learning of math skills. However, using calculators accurately is essential in many real-life situations. Encourage your child to use a calculator to complete homework or to help with household computations.

TALK ABOUT TESTS

Find out from your child's teacher when standardized tests will be given during the school year. Mark the dates on your calendar so that both you and your child know when test day approaches. Try not to schedule big activities for the night before a test.

To prepare for the yearly standardized test, score your child's work in this workbook together. Then talk about questions that were easy, hard, or tricky. Review any items answered incorrectly, and work together to understand why another answer is better.

A GOOD NIGHT'S SLEEP

Your child will be more relaxed and alert after a full night of sleep. Some physical exercise before dinner can relieve feelings of stress. Do not place too much emphasis on the upcoming test, but answer any questions your child may have and provide reassurance that your child is ready for the test. Reminders of what to expect may lower anxiety. Help your child choose clothing for the next day, and have it ready so there is no last-minute hunting in the morning.

FOOD FOR THOUGHT

Studies show a direct link between eating a balanced breakfast and student performance. Children who eat a good breakfast are alert in class, concentrate well, and recall information. These skills are useful at any time of the year, but are especially helpful on test day. To make sure your child eats a balanced breakfast, wake up early enough to leave plenty of time for a relaxed meal together.

SUPPORT YOUR CHILD

Remind your child that standardized tests measure learning. They do not measure intelligence. Supportive parents expect their children to do their best. Do not set specific goals or offer rewards for high scores. Instead, assure your child that you will be happy with a positive and wholehearted effort. Doing one's best is what really counts!

AFTER THE TEST

When your child comes home, discuss the testing experience. Do not focus on the test score. Instead, use the opportunity to reassure your child and talk about test-taking strategies. Ask your child which strategies were especially useful. To keep the mood relaxed at home, choose a fun activity to help your child unwind after the test.

When the test scores arrive, remember that they do not measure intelligence. They measure how well your child knows the materials and skills covered on that specific test.

Be sure to talk about the test score with your child. Remind your child that no single test score gives a complete picture of how much someone knows. Help your child set goals to maintain or improve test scores in the future. Always praise your child for working hard on a test. Test scores might suggest that your child needs improvement in a specific skill or subject. Talk with your child's teacher to find ways to support your child's growth in a particular area.

GET READY FOR TESTS

WHAT ARE STANDARDIZED TESTS?

You will take many different tests while at school. A standardized test is a special test that your state gives to every student in your grade. These tests are designed to find out how much you know about subjects like reading and math. They may not be fun, but they do not have to be a nightmare. This workbook can help you prepare!

WHAT CAN YOU EXPECT ON A STANDARDIZED TEST?

All standardized tests are different, but they do have some things in common.

- **Multiple-Choice Questions**
  Most of these tests use multiple-choice questions. You have to pick the best answer from four or five choices. You usually indicate your choice on an answer sheet by filling in or darkening a circle next to the correct answer.

- **Time Limits**
  Standardized tests all have time limits. It is best to answer as many questions as possible before you run out of time. But do not let the time limit make you nervous. Use it to help you keep going at a good pace.

- **Short Answers and Essays**
  Some standardized tests have questions that require writing an answer. Sometimes the answer is a word or a sentence. Other times you will write a paragraph or an essay. Always read directions carefully to find out how much writing is required.

HOW CAN THIS BOOK HELP?

Everyone gets a little nervous when taking a test. This book can make test-taking easier by providing helpful tips and practice tests. You will learn strategies that will help you find the best answers. You will also review math, reading, and grammar skills that are commonly needed on standardized tests. Here are some hints for using this book.

- Work in a quiet place. When you take a test at school, the room is very quiet. Try to copy that feeling at home. Sit in a chair at a desk or table, just as you would in school.

- Finish one test at a time. Do not try to finish all of the tests in this book in one session. It is better to complete just one activity at a time. You will learn more if you stop at the end of a practice test to think about the completed questions.

- Ask questions. Talk with a family member or a friend if you find a question you do not understand. These practice tests give you the chance to check your own answers.

Look for the Test Tips throughout this workbook. They provide hints and ideas to help you find the best answers.

A test-smart student knows what to do when it is test-taking time. You might not know all the answers, but you will feel relaxed and focused when you take tests. Your test scores will be accurate. They will provide a snapshot of what you have learned during the school year. Here is how you can become test-smart!

Things You Can Do All Year

The best way to get ready for tests is to pay attention in school every day. Do your homework. Be curious about the world around you. Learning takes place all the time, no matter where you are! When test day rolls around, you will be ready to show what you know. Here are some ways you can become a year-round learner.

- Do your schoolwork. Standardized tests measure how much you have learned. If you keep up with your schoolwork, your test scores will reflect all the things you have learned.

- Practice smart study habits. Most people study best when they work in a quiet, clean area. Keep your study area neat. Make sure you have a calculator, dictionary, paper, and pencils nearby.

- Read a wide variety of materials, including all sorts of fiction and nonfiction. Your school or local librarian can suggest books you might not have considered reading. Read newspapers and magazines to find out about current events.

- Practice. This book is a great start to help you get ready for test day. It provides practice for all the important skills on the tests.

How to Do Your Best on Test Day

Your teacher will announce a standardized test day in advance. Follow these tips to help you succeed on the big day.

- Plan a quiet night before a test. Trying to study or memorize facts at this point might make you nervous. Enjoy a relaxing evening instead.

- Go to bed on time. You need to be well rested before the test.

- Eat a balanced breakfast. Your body needs fuel to keep your energy high during a test. Eat foods that provide long-term energy, like eggs, yogurt, or fruit. Skip the sugary cereals—the energy they give does not last very long.

- Wear comfortable clothes. Choose a comfortable outfit that you like.

- Do not worry about the other students or your friends. Everyone works at different speeds. Pay attention to answering the questions in a steady fashion. It does not matter when someone else finishes the test.

- Relax. Take a few deep breaths to help you relax. Hold your pencil comfortably and do not squeeze it. Take a break every so often to wiggle your fingers and stretch your hand.

TEST-TAKING TIPS

Here are some hints and strategies to help you feel comfortable with any test. Remember these ideas while taking the tests in this book.

READ THE DIRECTIONS

This sounds obvious, but every year students lose points because they assume they know the right thing to do—and they are wrong! Make sure you read and understand the directions for every test. Always read the directions first. They will focus your attention on finding the right answers.

READ THE ANSWERS

Read the answers—ALL the answers—for a multiple-choice question, even if you think the first one is correct. Test writers sometimes include tricky answers that seem right when you first read them.

PREVIEW THE QUESTIONS

Scan each section. This will give you information about the questions. You also can see how many questions there are in the section. Do not spend too much time doing this. A quick glance will provide helpful information without making you nervous.

USE YOUR TIME WISELY

Always follow test rules. On most standardized tests, you can work on only one section at a time. Do not skip ahead or return to another section. If you finish early, go back and check your answers in that section.

- Before the test begins, find out if you can write in the test booklet. If so, add a small circle or star next to those questions that you find difficult. If time allows, come back to these questions before time is up for that section.

- Try not to spend too much time on one question. Skip a difficult question and try to answer it later. Be careful, though! You need to skip that question's number on your answer sheet. When you answer the next question, make sure you carefully fill in or darken the circle for the correct question.

- When finishing a section, look at your answer sheet. Did you answer every question for the section? Erase any extra marks on your answer sheet. Make sure you did not mark two answers for one question.

MAKE AN EDUCATED GUESS

Most standardized tests take away points for wrong answers. It might be wise to skip a question if you have no idea about the answer. Leave the answer blank and move on to the next question. But if you can eliminate one or more of the answers, guessing can be a great strategy. Remember, smart guessing can improve your test scores!

- Read every answer choice.

- Cross out every answer you know is wrong.

- Try rereading or restating the question to find the best answer.

THINK BEFORE YOU SWITCH

When you check your answers, you might be tempted to change one or more of them. In most cases, your first answer is probably the best choice. Ask yourself why you want to make a change. If you have a good reason, go ahead and pick a new answer. For example, you might have misread the question. If you cannot think of a specific reason, it is probably best to stick with your first answer.

FILL IN THE BLANKS

Many tests include fill-in-the-blank questions. The blank is usually in the middle or at the end of a sentence. Use these steps to answer a fill-in-the-blank question.

- Begin with the first answer choice. Read the sentence with that word or group of words in place of the blank. Ask yourself, "Does this answer make sense?"

- Then try filling in the blank with each of the other answer choices. Also, use the other words in the sentence as clues to help you decide the correct choice.

- Choose the best answer.

LOOK FOR CLUE WORDS

When you read test questions, watch for *clue words* that provide important information. Here are some words that make a difference.

- NOT: Many questions ask you to find the answer that is not true. These questions can be tricky. Slow down and think about the meaning of the question. Then pick the one answer that is not true.

- ALWAYS, NEVER, ALL, NONE, ONLY: These words limit a statement. They often make a generally true statement into a false one.

- SOMETIMES, SOME, MOST, MANY, OFTEN, GENERALLY: These words make a statement more believable. You will find them in many correct answers.

- BEST, MOST LIKELY, SAME, OPPOSITE, PROBABLY: These words change the meaning of a sentence. You often can use them to eliminate choices.

RESTATE THE QUESTION

Short answer or essay questions require writing an answer. Your response must answer the question. Restate the question to make sure your answer stays on target. For example, if the question is "What causes lightning?" your answer should begin with the words "Lightning is caused by . . ."

TEST TIP

Be sure to look for the Test Tips throughout this workbook. They will give you more test-taking strategies and specific help with certain subject areas.

UNIT 2
SIX READING SKILLS

Prefixes and suffixes are parts of some words. A prefix appears at the beginning of a word. A suffix appears at the end of a word. Both prefixes and suffixes affect the meaning of words. You can use them to help figure out the meaning of a word.

Mount Mazama is a volcano in Oregon. It has been <u>inactive</u> for years. The edges of the crater have fallen in. The crater has filled up with water. It is now known as Crater Lake.

1 **In this paragraph, the word <u>inactive</u> means —**

A   upset.

B   quiet.

C   alive.

D   stubborn.

Hint: "In-" is a prefix. It means not.

The porcupine fish can make itself look very odd. If it senses danger, it takes a breath of air and puffs out its body. Then it looks like a spine-covered ball. When the danger passes, the fish <u>deflates</u> itself.

2 **What happens when a balloon <u>deflates</u>?**

The air gets let out &
it shrinks

Hint: "De-" is a prefix. It means to reverse the action of, or to undo.

The Maya Indians once built great cities. They lived in an area that stretched from southern Mexico to Central America. Then the Maya began to <u>evacuate</u> the large cities. They moved to farms or small towns. The reason they left the cities is still unknown.

3 **In this paragraph, the word <u>evacuate</u> means —**

F   sweep.

G   build.

H   join.

J   leave.

Hint: "E-" is a prefix. It means out.

When John found the stray cat, its fur was so wet and dirty that he could see its ribs. He tried to give it some milk, but it was too sick to drink any. He could not bear to watch it <u>suffering</u> and took it to the animal shelter.

4 **In this paragraph, the word <u>suffering</u> means —**

A   drooling.

B   experiencing pain.

C   having stitches.

D   experiencing pleasure.

Hint: The suffix "-ing" means the act of.

GO ON

Answers

1 Ⓐ B Ⓒ Ⓓ   3 Ⓕ G Ⓗ J   4 Ⓐ B Ⓒ Ⓓ

Sometimes you can figure out the meaning of a new or difficult word by using the words around it as clues.

Have you ever seen a sea monster? People in northern Scotland believe a sea monster lives in Loch Ness, a nearby lake. Many people have reported seeing the creature. <u>Observers</u> say that it has flippers, a hump, and a long, thin neck.

5 **In this paragraph, the word <u>observers</u> means —**

F police.

(G) watchers.

H campers.

J doctors.

Hint: You get a clue about what the word means by reading sentences 3 and 4.

Bedrich Smetana wrote music. When he was fifty years old, he became totally deaf. But he did not let this <u>check</u> his interest in music. He wrote some of his finest pieces after going deaf.

6 **In this paragraph, the word <u>check</u> means —**

A mark.

B nail.

(C) stop.

D open.

Hint: You get a clue about what the word means by reading sentences 3 and 4.

The space shuttle needs extra power to be launched. To get this power, the shuttle is connected to a large fuel <u>reservoir</u> and two rocket boosters. These fall off as the shuttle climbs into space.

7 **What is a fuel <u>reservoir</u>?**

a big reserve, or place to keep things

Hint: You get a clue about what the word <u>reservoir</u> means by reading sentences 1 and 2.

Many plants grow in places that do not have the minerals they need. The plants must <u>adapt</u> to their surroundings. One of these plants is the pitcher plant. It traps and eats insects for the minerals it needs to grow properly.

8 **In this paragraph, the word <u>adapt</u> means —**

F enjoy.

G answer.

(H) adjust.

J hatch.

Hint: You get a clue about what the word <u>adapt</u> means by reading sentences 1 and 2.

GO ON

Answers
5 (F) (G) (H) (J)   6 (A) (B) (C) (D)   8 (F) (G) (H) (J)

13

Specialized or technical words are words used in specific subjects, such as science and social studies. You can use all the other information in the text to help determine the meaning of these words.

Most animals use some kind of <u>respiration</u> to stay alive. A water spider gets air from large bubbles in the water. Whales, however, must come to the surface of the water to get air for their lungs.

9   In this paragraph the word <u>respiration</u> means —

    A food.

    B breathing.

    C water.

    D trick.

Hint: The word respiration *is a technical word. You get a clue about what it means by reading the entire paragraph.*

Plants can be attacked by insects or destroyed by bad weather. Sometimes plants are struck by an <u>epidemic</u>. Then many plants get sick and die.

10   What is an <u>epidemic</u>?

_____

_____

_____

Hint: Epidemic *is a technical word. You get a clue about what it means by reading the entire paragraph.*

The moon appears to change its shape over a period of about thirty days. For that reason the moon can be used to measure the passing of time. That's why people long ago developed <u>lunar</u> calendars.

11   In this paragraph the word <u>lunar</u> means —

    F of the time.

    G of long ago.

    H of the moon.

    J of the people.

Hint: <u>Lunar</u> *is a technical word. You get a clue about what it means by reading the entire paragraph.*

TEST TIP

Remember that many words have more than one meaning. Technical words have special meanings in certain subject areas. For example, the word *work* has a technical meaning in science. *Work* is "the energy used when a force moves an object."

When you read test passages, take a moment to identify the subject area. If it is a science or social studies topic, slow down and be alert for this kind of technical term.

GO ON

Answers
  9 Ⓐ Ⓑ Ⓒ Ⓓ **11** Ⓕ Ⓖ Ⓗ Ⓙ

On July 11, 1991, the people in Hawaii had a thrilling experience. The Earth, moon, and sun lined up. This made the sun seem to disappear. This eclipse of the sun lasted over seven minutes.

12 **In this paragraph the word eclipse means —**

A darkening.

B coloring.

C brightness.

D heat.

Hint: The word eclipse is a technical term. You get a clue about what eclipse means by reading sentences 2 and 3.

Richard Leakey was born in Kenya, Africa, in 1944. He has found many important fossils of early humans. He discovered some skulls that are thought to be over one million years old!

13 **In this paragraph the word fossils means —**

F bones.

G dinosaurs.

H tribes.

J photographs.

Hint: The word fossils is a technical term. You get a clue about what fossils means by reading sentences 2 and 3.

When ducks migrate south each fall, many of them pass over Stuttgard, Arkansas. So the people there hold a duck-calling contest. As the ducks fly by, the people quack away!

14 **What does the word migrate mean in this paragraph?**

_____

_____

_____

_____

Hint: The word migrate is a technical term. You get a clue about what the word migrate means by reading the entire paragraph.

TEST TIP

When you have to provide a short answer, choose your words carefully. Try to write an answer that gets right to the point. You do not need to impress people with fancy words. Simply give your answer as directly and completely as possible.

STOP

Answers
12 (A) (B) (C) (D)   **13** (F) (G) (H) (J)

15

Facts or details are important. By noticing and remembering them, you will know what the passage is about.

Do you think that the North Pole and the South Pole are alike? Most people do. But in fact the two areas are quite different. The North Pole is in the Arctic Ocean. The South Pole lies near the center of Antarctica. Antarctica is colder than the Arctic. In fact, Antarctica is by far the coldest region on earth.

One reason for Antarctica's very cold climate is that it has mountains high above sea level. Summers there rarely get above freezing. Ice and snow cover almost all of Antarctica throughout the entire year.

The Arctic region includes lands around the Arctic Ocean. The Arctic region is mostly at or near sea level. In parts of the Arctic, summers can be as warm as those in Boston. They just do not last as long. Most of the Arctic lands have no snow or ice in the summer.

1   The Arctic is mostly —

   A   in Boston.

   B   at sea level.

   C   above sea level.

   D   below sea level.

   Hint: Look at paragraph 3.

2   Antarctica has —

   F   rivers.

   G   sand.

   H   mountains.

   J   jungles.

   Hint: The fact is in the story.

3   The North Pole is —

   A   on land.

   B   on a mountain.

   C   in the Arctic Ocean.

   D   in Antarctica.

   Hint: Look at sentence 4.

Antarctica has most of the world's permanent ice. The ice rests on land. Its average thickness is 8,000 feet. But ice in the Arctic rests on water. Its thickness varies from 10 to 65 feet.

If you traveled to the Arctic, you would see reindeer, polar bears, seals, birds, and insects. If your stay lasted through all the seasons, you might see over a thousand types of plants. You might also meet some of the people who live there. These people have learned to live in the cold climate quite well. They have been able to use the plants and animals there. Most of the people live near the sea, where they catch fish.

If you visited Antarctica, you would see ice and more ice. Very few animals and plants can live there. Most animals live on the coast. The largest animal that can live on the mainland is a small fly. And you would not see people at all, unless you ran into an explorer or scientist.

4   What does the Arctic ice rest on?

   _____

   _____

   _____

   _____

   Hint: Look for the sentence about Arctic ice.

GO ON ➡

Answers
   1 Ⓐ Ⓑ Ⓒ Ⓓ   2 Ⓕ Ⓖ Ⓗ Ⓙ   3 Ⓐ Ⓑ Ⓒ Ⓓ

Sometimes it is helpful to arrange events in the order they happened. This may help you to understand a passage better.

Giraffes are the tallest living animals. Most adult giraffes are tall enough to look into second-story windows. Their long necks help them get leaves and fruit that no other animal can reach. Let's see how a giraffe's life begins.

A female giraffe, or cow, gives birth to a baby 15 months after mating. The mother searches for a safe place to give birth. Both the baby, or calf, and the mother are in a great deal of danger right after the birth. More than half of all baby giraffes are killed by lions, cheetahs, or hyenas minutes after they are born.

The new baby drops the 5 feet from its mother to the ground with a thud. It weighs about 130 pounds and is 6 feet tall. The baby can run and jump 10 hours after it is born, but it cannot outrun an enemy.

The mother hides the calf in tall grass. Then she goes to search for food. The baby is safe as long as it stays still. The cow returns to nurse the baby. The calf stays hidden for about a month.

After a month the mother and baby join a group of four or five other cows with their calves. The calves stay together while their mothers gather food. Sometimes one mother stays with them. The cows return at night to protect the calves. The calves stay in this group until they are about a year old.

By the time they are a year old, the giraffes are 10 to 12 feet tall. They can outrun all of their enemies except the cheetah. The giraffes rarely attack an animal larger than themselves. They continue to grow until they are 7 or 8 years old. Adults are between 14 and 18 feet tall.

5 **Which happens first in the story?**

F   The mother joins a group.

G   The mother hides the calf.

H   The mother searches for a safe place.

J   The mother searches for food.

Hint: Look at the beginning.

6 **When does a female giraffe give birth?**

A   after she joins a group of other cows

B   every 15 months

C   15 months after mating

D   every year

Hint: Look at paragraph 2.

7 **When are the mother and baby in greatest danger?**

_____

_____

_____

_____

Hint: Look at paragraph 2.

8 **When do the cow and calf join a group?**

F   about a month after the baby is born

G   when the calf is a year old

H   when the calf is 7 or 8 years old

J   10 to 12 months after the baby is born

Hint: Look at paragraph 5.

9 **When do giraffes stop growing?**

A   when they are 10 or 12 years old

B   when they are 7 or 8 years old

C   when they join a group of other giraffes

D   when they are 14 to 18 years old

Hint: Look at the second to last sentence in the selection.

GO ON ➡

Answers

5 Ⓕ Ⓖ Ⓗ Ⓙ   **6** Ⓐ Ⓑ Ⓒ Ⓓ   **8** Ⓕ Ⓖ Ⓗ Ⓙ   **9** Ⓐ Ⓑ Ⓒ Ⓓ

Written directions tell you how to do something. To follow them means to do them in the same order in which they are given.

Linda left a note for her daughter, because school was starting the next day. In the note she said, "Erin, take the list of supplies you need down to the stationery store. I left $20 on the kitchen counter for you. Put the money and your house key in your pocket. Please walk so you don't have to worry about your bicycle while you shop. Get as many of the items on the list as you can. We'll get the rest after I get home from work. If you have any money left over, you can get a soda at the luncheonette next door. Please be careful, and don't buy candy!"

10   What is Erin to do after she puts the $20 in her pocket?

F   ride her bicycle

G   leave a note for her mother

H   walk to the store

J   put her house key in her pocket

Hint: Find the part of the directions about putting the money in her pocket and read what comes after that.

Peggy Johnson is a firefighter. When she arrived at midnight for her eight-hour shift, she found instructions from her new supervisor:

Sign in. Inspect engine 5 first. After making sure it is running well, be sure that it has plenty of gas. Inspect the hats, coats, and other firefighting equipment. If you have time before your 4:00 A.M. meal break, inspect engine 1 and check the gas tank on that engine as well. I hope that you will not be called out on any fire and can use the rest of your shift to fill out next week's work schedules for the rest of the crew. See you at 8:00 A.M.!

11   When should Peggy inspect engine 5?

_____

_____

_____

Hint: Find the sentence that directs Peggy to inspect engine 5.

TEST TIP

Time order is also called *chronological order*. Pay close attention to dates and times, as well as signal words that tell about time, such as:

first	next
then	finally
before	after
since	lastly

You might circle these words in the test passage to help you decide the order of events.

 GO ON

Answers
10 Ⓕ Ⓖ Ⓗ Ⓙ

The setting of a story lets you know when and where it is taking place.

Chimney sweeps have been around for hundreds of years. Chimneys had to be cleaned or the fireplaces would not work properly. Dirty chimneys could cause fires. Many countries passed laws that required chimneys to be cleaned once or twice a year. Chimney sweeping became a regular profession.

Life was hard for chimney sweeps in England in the 1700s. Tall, narrow houses were built in the cities. Chimneys were designed to take up as little space as possible. They were too small for adults to climb into. So, many sweeps hired young boys as helpers, or apprentices. These boys were not treated well. They spent long hours climbing into dirty chimneys. Most of the time, they were not given enough warm food or warm clothing. In 1788 a law was passed that said sweeps could not be younger than eight.

12   What were houses like in English cities in the 1700s?

   A   They were dirty and rundown.

   B   They had no chimneys.

   C   They were tall and narrow with small chimneys.

   D   They were large with small chimneys.

   Hint: Find the description of the English houses.

13   What century is the passage about?

   F   16th century

   G   17th century

   H   18th century

   J   19th century

   Hint: Look for a date.

Would you like to step back in time? If so, you might enjoy a trip to Mesa Verde National Park. Mesa Verde is in southwestern Colorado. Spanish explorers gave this region its name. Mesa verde means "green plateau." It became a national park in 1906.

Scientists have studied the region and have learned a great deal about the people who lived there. They called them the Anasazi, or "old ones." We know that about the year 1200 the Anasazi built their homes in the caves of the canyon walls. They used stone blocks to build apartment-like dwellings. When you see them, it is easy to pretend you are one of the people who lived there centuries ago.

14   The Anasazi built their homes —

   A   about 1906.

   B   about 1200.

   C   about 1900.

   D   about 600 years ago.

   Hint: Read paragraph 2, sentence 3.

15   Where does the story take place?

   _____

   _____

   _____

   _____

   Hint: Read sentence 3.

STOP

Answers
12 Ⓐ Ⓑ Ⓒ Ⓓ   **13** Ⓕ Ⓖ Ⓗ Ⓙ   **14** Ⓐ Ⓑ Ⓒ Ⓓ

The main idea is the overall meaning of a piece of writing. Often the main idea is written in the passage.

When Millard Fillmore was nineteen, he could hardly read or write. He lived on a farm. He spent more time working than going to school. But later he decided to return to school. Abigail Powers was Fillmore's teacher. They fell in love, and later they were married. Fillmore went on to become a teacher, a lawyer, and the President of the United States!

1   What is the main idea of this story?

   A   Fillmore achieved great things after being educated.

   B   Fillmore went to school as a boy.

   C   Fillmore taught Abigail to read.

   D   Fillmore never married.

   Hint: What is the point of the story?

In 1692 some girls in Massachusetts decided that they did not like their neighbors. So the girls accused the neighbors of being witches. The girls said they were cut, pinched, and choked by strange visitors who looked like their neighbors. Many people were arrested, and twenty people were put to death. But one man accused of being a wizard said he would file a lawsuit against the girls. Then the girls took back their lies.

2   What is the main idea of the story?

   F   The girls disliked normal people.

   G   Some girls caused trouble in their town.

   H   A man threatening to file a lawsuit put an end to the girls' lies.

   J   Witchcraft trials were held in Massachusetts.

   Hint: What does the whole story talk about?

Frederic Bartholdi was the French sculptor of the Statue of Liberty. When Bartholdi was a student in France, a wall was built to keep out the enemy. One night a girl carrying a torch jumped over the wall and yelled, "Forward!" The enemy soldiers shot her. Years later Bartholdi remembered the girl with the torch in her hand. It gave him an idea. Bartholdi used his wife as the model for the shape of the statue. His mother served as the model for the statue's face.

3   What is this story mostly about?

   _____

   _____

   _____

   _____

   Hint: What is the whole story about?

In 1174 work began on the bell tower of a church in Pisa, Italy. Because the foundation of the tower was laid in soil that was too soft, it began to lean. Work on the tower stopped. For more than one hundred years, people suggested ways to prevent the tower from leaning. The building was finished in 1350, but it continued to sink. Each year the tower leans a little more. Tourists today still visit the famous Leaning Tower of Pisa.

4   The main idea of this story is that the Leaning Tower of Pisa —

   A   had been leaning from its beginning.

   B   was poorly built.

   C   is one of many bell towers.

   D   has many visitors.

   Hint: What is the whole story about?

GO ON

Answers

1 Ⓐ Ⓑ Ⓒ Ⓓ   **2** Ⓕ Ⓖ Ⓗ Ⓙ   **4** Ⓐ Ⓑ Ⓒ Ⓓ

Often the main idea is not given in the text. Sometimes you need to draw your own conclusion by putting the facts together.

Chip's family was at the beach. His grandmother had planned to come but couldn't because she was ill. Chip remembered how she would let him look at her shell collection when he was younger. He used to enjoy holding the big conch shell up to his ear to hear the sound of the sea. The day before his family planned to return home, Chip went out early in the morning and picked up several interesting shells for his grandmother.

5   What is the main idea of this passage?

F   Chip always enjoyed going to the beach with his family.

G   Chip's grandmother was always getting sick and disappointing Chip.

H   Chip wanted his grandmother to know he was thinking of her.

J   Chip's grandmother collected seashells.

Hint: What point does the story make?

The first pair of roller skates was made in 1760 by Joseph Merlin. Merlin tried to sell his skates in London, but he didn't have much success. One problem was that they didn't have brakes! That problem was soon solved, and more people began trying the new sport. But it wasn't until 1849 that the sport caught on. That year a play was held in which actors were supposed to ice skate. But they could not make ice on stage. So the actors used roller skates instead.

6   What is the implied main idea?

A   The sport of roller skating was made popular by a stage play.

B   Roller skating will never become a very popular sport.

C   Merlin made the first pair of skates.

D   Skates are dangerous without brakes.

Hint: Think about what the passage is about. Which choice best sums it up?

Martin loved dogs. He asked his parents for a golden retriever. His parents agreed to get him a dog for his birthday if he promised to take care of it. Martin quickly agreed. He named the dog Calvin. The first few weeks, Martin took Calvin out for a walk twice a day. He kept his bowl filled with water and fed him each evening. But after two months, Martin's parents noticed that the water bowl was often empty and that Calvin had not been fed.

7   What is the main idea of this passage?

_____

_____

_____

_____

Hint: What is the point of the story?

TEST TIP

When you want to find the main idea of a test passage, ask yourself, "What is this passage mostly about?" The *main idea* should describe the big idea of a passage, not specific details.

Sometimes the main idea is stated in a topic sentence, often at the beginning of a paragraph. Other times, you will need to figure out the main idea of a passage. Try to name the big idea supported by the paragraph's details.

GO ON

Answers
5 Ⓕ Ⓖ Ⓗ Ⓙ   **6** Ⓐ Ⓑ Ⓒ Ⓓ

A good summary contains the main idea of a passage. It is brief, yet it covers the most important points.

Do you ever wonder how games are invented? James Naismith was teaching a physical education class when he accidentally made up a new game. He combined the games of lacrosse and soccer. But the players neither used a stick as in lacrosse nor kicked a ball as in soccer. Instead they bounced, or dribbled, the ball and shot at a goal. The only thing Naismith had to use as a goal was a peach basket. This is why he decided to call his game basketball.

8   What is this story mostly about?

F   Most people can learn lacrosse.

G   Naismith taught physical education.

H   New games can be invented by accident.

J   Soccer and lacrosse are different.

Hint: Look at sentences 1 and 2.

It is possible to eat healthy food at a fast-food restaurant. You could drink orange juice or low-fat milk instead of a malt or a milk shake. You could try a whole-grain bun rather than the regular white one on your sandwich. A baked potato instead of fried potatoes would be a healthy choice. But you'll need to have the potato plain rather than with all the trimmings.

9   What is the best summary of this passage?

A   The most popular fast foods are healthy foods.

B   There are healthy ways to eat at fast-food restaurants.

C   All fast food is junk food.

D   Fried potatoes are a healthy choice.

Hint: Which choice tells you about the whole passage?

There are about 2,000 kinds of snakes in the world. They live on land, in the ground, in water, and in trees. About 120 types of snakes are found in the United States. But only four types are actually poisonous. These are the coral snake, rattlesnake, copperhead, and water moccasin. The coral snake lives mainly in the South. Rattlesnakes are found in most states. The copperhead lives mostly in the East, while the water moccasin can be found in the Southeast.

10   What is this story mostly about?

_____

_____

_____

_____

_____

Hint: Which sentences tell you about the whole passage?

TEST TIP

When you read the answer choices for question 9, notice some of the signal words that make answers incorrect. Answer A includes the word *most* and answer C includes the word *all*. These strong adjectives often make a sentence false. The correct answer to this question tells about the whole passage and makes a less extreme statement.

 GO ON

Answers
8 Ⓕ Ⓖ Ⓗ Ⓙ   **9** Ⓐ Ⓑ Ⓒ Ⓓ

Colorblindness has to do with a person's lack of ability to see colors. But it doesn't affect a person's sight. People with full-color vision have three kinds of cone-shaped cells in their eyes. One kind of cone sees red, another sees green, and the third kind of cone sees blue. A person who is colorblind is missing one or more of these kinds of cones. Red-green colorblindness is the most common. People with this kind of colorblindness see red or green as gray-brown. They don't have red or green cones.

11   What is this story mostly about?

F   If people are missing certain cone-shaped cells in their eyes, they are colorblind.

G   There are a number of people who are colorblind.

H   Red-blue colorblindness is very common.

J   People who are colorblind wear glasses.

Hint: Read sentences 3 and 5.

Which kind of clam chowder do you prefer? In the United States, there are two kinds of clam chowder. Manhattan clam chowder is made with tomatoes. New England clam chowder is made with milk. People from Massachusetts take their clam chowder very seriously. They even passed a law that does not allow clam chowder with tomatoes in their state!

12   What is the best summary of this passage?

A   There is a difference between New Englanders and other people.

B   There are different kinds of clam chowders.

C   Clam chowder is a kind of soup.

D   There is only one way to make clam chowder.

Hint: Pick the choice that sums up the passage.

During the 1850s, Levi Strauss moved to San Francisco. He sold canvas material used for making tents and covered wagons. Gold miners and railroad workers complained that their pants tore easily or wore out too soon. So Strauss used his canvas to make a pair of pants. He named the pants after himself. They sold for 22 cents a pair. Later Strauss made a pair of denim pants, dyed them blue, and named them Levi's also.

13   What is this passage mostly about?

_____

_____

_____

_____

_____

_____

Hint: Read sentences 4, 5, and 7.

TEST TIP

A good summary should give the main idea of a passage without focusing on specific details. A summary should not be too general, though. As you read the answer choices for question 12, you will notice that answer C is too general. It makes a true statement, but it does not really tell about the passage.

STOP

Answers
11 Ⓕ Ⓖ Ⓗ Ⓙ   **12** Ⓐ Ⓑ Ⓒ Ⓓ

Knowing what made something happen or why a character did something will help you to understand what you read.

The telephone rang sharply in the middle of the night. Missy sat upright in her bed, rubbing her eyes. Again the sharp ringing split the silence. Trying to pull herself together, Missy scrambled for the phone. She had no idea who could be calling at that time of night, but she hoped it was not an emergency. When she answered the phone, a voice at the other end asked for someone named Felix. Disgusted, Missy said that Felix did not live there. Then the person on the other end slammed down the phone.

1   Why did Missy rub her eyes?

_____

_____

_____

_____

_____

Hint: Rubbing her eyes is the effect. What made this happen?

2   What caused Missy to hope that it was not an emergency?

A   The sound of the telephone was sharp.

B   She associated the voice on the phone with trouble.

C   The call came in the middle of the night.

D   She tore her nightclothes trying to scramble for the phone.

Hint: The effect was hoping that it was not an emergency. What caused Missy to hope that?

3   Why was Missy disgusted?

F   She did not like the name Felix.

G   She did not like to be awakened by someone calling the wrong number.

H   The person calling slammed down the phone.

J   She did not know who was calling.

Hint: Being disgusted is the effect. What made this happen?

Emma Willard worked hard for women's rights. In the early nineteenth century, she came up with a plan to improve schools for women. She felt that a woman could master any subject that a man could. So she offered a wide range of subjects at her school. She trained many young women to be teachers.

4   Which of the following did not cause Emma Willard to want to improve schools for women?

A   She believed that women could master any subject men could.

B   She wanted women to have a wider range of subjects to choose from.

C   She wanted to train young women to be teachers.

D   She wanted to make women better than men.

Hint: Improving schools for women is the effect. What was NOT one of Emma's reasons for wanting to improve schools?

GO ON

Answers

2 ⒶⒷⒸⒹ   3 ⒻⒼⒽⒿ   4 ⒶⒷⒸⒹ

Michael liked the cool, crisp fall weather so much that he actually enjoyed raking leaves. One day he noticed that Mr. Longly's yard down the road was full of leaves. Michael knew that Mr. Longly used a wheelchair to get around. That day after school, Michael picked up his rake and headed for Mr. Longly's house.

5   Why did Michael go to Mr. Longly's house?

    F He planned on raking Mr. Longly's leaves, since Mr. Longly couldn't do it himself.

    G He liked fall better than the other seasons.

    H He didn't want to go inside.

    J He enjoyed raking leaves so much that he went looking for some more.

Hint: Read each choice and decide which makes the most sense.

Patty and her mom were very excited about planting their first garden. They looked forward to growing their own vegetables. First they used a hoe to prepare the soil. Then they added peat moss to the soil. They planted tomatoes, lettuce, beans, and peas. Every week Patty spent at least an hour weeding and watering the plants. At the end of the summer, Patty shared the vegetables with her friends.

6   Why was Patty excited about planting a garden?

_____

_____

_____

_____

_____

Hint: Getting excited about planting a garden is the effect. What caused Patty to get excited?

TEST TIP

When a question begins with the word *why*, you need to find a cause-and-effect relationship to answer it. The effect is what happens; the cause is the reason why it happens. You can use the word *because* to answer a question that asks *why*. Begin your response to question 6 by writing "Patty was excited about planting a garden because . . ."

GO ON

Answers
5 Ⓕ Ⓖ Ⓗ Ⓙ

Many times you can predict, or tell in advance, what is probably going to happen next. You must think about what would make sense if the story were to go on.

Ruth's hobby was making radio-controlled airplanes. But even more than making them, she enjoyed flying the planes. Once Ruth spent every weekend for an entire month working with her dad to build an airplane. The next Saturday Ruth decided to try out the plane. When Ruth set up the airplane for takeoff, she didn't notice the tall pine trees standing in its path.

7   What might happen next?

    A Ruth and her father will cut down the trees.

    B The airplane will crash into the trees.

    C Ruth's father will finish building the airplane.

    D Ruth will get a ticket for flying an airplane without a license.

Hint: You need to look at all the facts in the story. What choice makes the most sense?

James and Jenny wanted to give their mom a special birthday present. "I have an idea," James said. "We could clean the whole house from top to bottom." "You're right! Mom would never believe it!" Jenny said. The next Saturday they asked their dad to take their mom out all afternoon. They vacuumed, dusted, and washed floors and windows until the whole house sparkled.

8   What will happen when James' and Jenny's mom gets home?

_____

_____

_____

_____

_____

Hint: You need to read the entire paragraph.

TEST TIP

When a test asks you to predict what will happen next, do not try to think of a creative or weird event that *could* happen. Your goal should be to answer with something that is likely to happen.

Look at question 8. The test writers want to know what is the most likely thing to happen, not the most unusual or funniest event. Think about the clues in the paragraph. How do you think their mom will react to the clean house?

GO ON

Answers

7 Ⓐ Ⓑ Ⓒ Ⓓ

"A package came for you today," Greg's mother said as he walked into the house. "I think it's from Aunt Ginny." Greg peeled the tape from the box and ripped off the brown paper. He tore off the gift wrap to find a stuffed bear inside. Aunt Ginny never seemed to realize that he was no longer three years old and hadn't been for over seven years. But then, he thought about the trouble Aunt Ginny had gone through to select the present and mail it. Greg sat down at the kitchen table with a pen and paper.

9 **What will Greg probably do next?**

_____

_____

_____

_____

Hint: What is the paragraph mostly about? The answer will be about that, too.

Each summer Jackie visited her grandparents on their farm for two weeks. She loved feeding the ducks on the pond. In the early evening, after a hot day of working in the fields, she took some bread to the pond. The ducks swam quickly to gobble up the bread she threw in the water. She watched the clear water reflect the bright colors of the sun as it disappeared beyond the horizon.

10 **What did Jackie probably do next?**

F camp out by the pond

G start a campfire

H go to the store for more bread

J go back to the farmhouse

Hint: Which of the choices would most likely come next?

TEST TIP

Remember that the word *probably* is a clue that helps you pick an answer. In question 10, all of the answer choices are possible, but only one of them is the most likely thing to happen. Notice that there is nothing in the story about camping. Therefore, you have no reason to think that Jackie will decide to camp out. The story begins in the early evening, so what is she most likely to do after the sun sets?

STOP

Answers
10 Ⓕ Ⓖ Ⓗ Ⓙ

Sometimes a passage will have a graph or diagram with it. These are there to help you understand the passage.

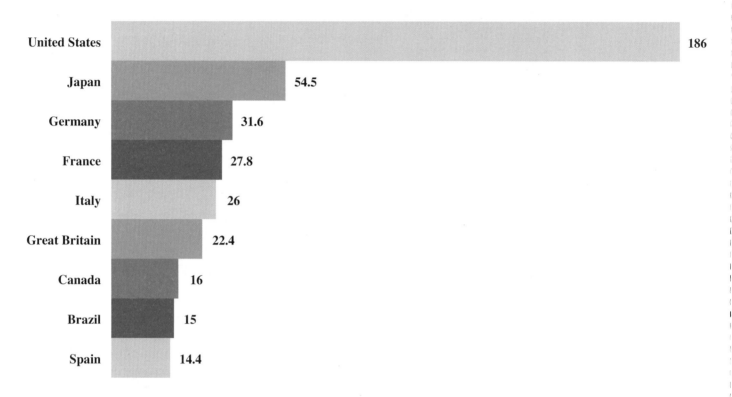

**NUMBER OF PASSENGER CARS
PER COUNTRY IN MILLIONS (1990)**

United States	186
Japan	54.5
Germany	31.6
France	27.8
Italy	26
Great Britain	22.4
Canada	16
Brazil	15
Spain	14.4

France has an excellent railroad system. Despite this fine system, the French still prefer to travel by car. There are 27.8 million cars on the road in France. If all these vehicles were placed end to end, the line would stretch four times around the world. Only the United States, Japan, and Germany have more vehicles than France.

1 **According to the graph, which country has the most cars?**

A Japan

B Germany

C France

D United States

Hint: Which bar on the graph is the longest?

2 **How many cars were there in France in 1990?**

_____

_____

_____

_____

_____

_____

Hint: Look at the bar labeled "France."

GO ON

Answers
1 Ⓐ Ⓑ Ⓒ Ⓓ

28

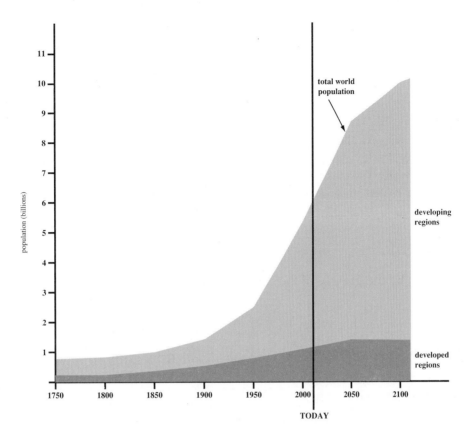

There are more people in the world than ever before. This is because people all over the world are living longer. More people have clean water. We have medicine to fight many illnesses. People are eating better than ever before. However, scientists think that this population growth will slow down by the year 2050.

3 **According to the graph, what is the total world population today?**

_____

_____

_____

_____

_____

_____

Hint: Find the place where the "today" line crosses with the "total world population."

4 **According to the graph, what can be said about the world population?**

F The population of the developed regions is greater today than that of the developing regions.

G The population of the developing regions is greater today than that of the developed regions.

H The population of the developing regions today is equal to that of the developed regions.

J The population of the developing regions is decreasing.

Hint: Check each choice against the graph.

Answers
4 Ⓕ Ⓖ Ⓗ Ⓙ

A logical conclusion is an ending that makes sense. Many times it can be proved by the information given in the paragraph.

Seashores experience a daily change in water level. This change is called tide. As the water is pulled from the shore, the water level drops. This is known as low tide. As the water returns to shore, the water level rises. This is called high tide. The coming and going of the water is caused by the pull of the moon's gravity.

5   **You can conclude that —**

   A   tides are caused by the gravity of the sun.

   B   the water level drops at high tide.

   C   the moon has a strong effect on Earth's seas.

   D   a tide is a change in water temperature.

   Hint: Read the last sentence to draw the proper conclusion.

Carbon dioxide in the atmosphere acts as a blanket. It lets light pass through, but it traps heat. This occurrence is called the greenhouse effect. It is good, for without it the earth would be much colder. But as the carbon dioxide increases, the heat of the earth's surface rises. This isn't good. Carbon dioxide comes from the burning of oil, coal, and gasoline. If we do not limit this burning, the world may suffer as a result.

6   **From the passage you can tell that —**

   F   carbon dioxide traps light.

   G   the earth would be warmer without the greenhouse effect.

   H   the greenhouse effect is never good.

   J   too much carbon dioxide is bad.

   Hint: You must read the entire paragraph, especially sentences 5 and 6.

Why do some dogs bark all the time? Some experts believe that dogs communicate through their barking. Other experts believe that dogs bark just to make noise. A new study supports this second view. The study suggests that dogs are wolves that just never grew up. Although dogs and wolves have the same ancestors, modern dogs behave in much the same ways as wolf pups, which bark all the time. However, older wolves seldom bark.

7   **From the passage you can tell that —**

   A   all experts agree on why dogs bark.

   B   a study supports the claim that dogs bark to communicate.

   C   old wolves bark all the time.

   D   a study suggests that dogs bark just to make noise

   Hint: Pick the choice that can be proved true by what's in the passage.

TEST TIP

If you have trouble finding an answer, first cross off any answer choices you know are incorrect. Then keep the remaining answer choices in mind as you reread the paragraph. Look for clues in the paragraph to help you decide which answer makes the most sense.

GO ON ➡

Answers

5   Ⓐ Ⓑ Ⓒ Ⓓ   6   Ⓕ Ⓖ Ⓗ Ⓙ   7   Ⓐ Ⓑ Ⓒ Ⓓ

By noting a person's physical changes, a lie detector machine shows whether someone is lying. The machine shows changes in heartbeat and breathing. These changes might take place when a person is lying. But these changes also take place when a person is nervous. Sometimes a person is lying but doesn't know it. In this case the machine doesn't note any change at all.

8 **From this selection, you cannot tell —**

F   what happens when a person lies.

G   what a lie detector shows.

H   which changes take place when a person is nervous.

J   how a lie detector is used in court.

Hint: You need to read the entire selection to see what you cannot tell.

The porcupine uses the quills on its tail to defend itself. When an animal comes too close, the porcupine slaps its tail at the enemy. The sharp quills come off easily. They stick into the other creature's skin. Each quill has a hook at the end. This makes the quills very painful to remove from the skin.

9 **If porcupines did not have quills, they would —**

A   use claws for defense.

B   be unable to defend themselves.

C   build dams with their tails.

D   find it painful.

Hint: First, cross out the choices that cannot be supported by the information in the passage.

Inventors record their inventions with the government. The inventors hope that someone will buy their bright ideas. But some inventions are so strange that no one wants them. Government files show inventions for odd things, such as flying fire escapes and eyeglasses for chickens. There is even an alarm clock that hits the sleeping person on the head.

10 **What type of inventions are described in this story?**

_____

_____

_____

_____

_____

Hint: Read the first three sentences to draw the proper conclusion.

TEST TIP

Always read a question carefully. Notice that question 10 asks, "What *type* of inventions is described in this story?" This is a very different question from "What inventions are described in this story?" You could answer the second question with a list of inventions. The first question, however, asks you to make a generalization. You need to explain what all of the inventions described in the story have in common.

GO ON

Answers
8 F G H J   **9** A B C D

The way a person acts tells you about the character's mood. Other clues may be what is said or how the character responds to what happens in the passage.

Alur had a beautiful wife and four cheerful children, and there were never any quarrels in his home. One day Alur visited his old friend Gungu. Gungu was smoking a pipe, which was an unusual thing for him to do. "Why are you smoking a pipe?" asked Alur. "Well, my friend," answered Gungu, "the smoke from this pipe carries my troubles away."

Alur asked, "What is trouble? I've never heard of it. It sounds exciting and interesting. I would like to obtain some of this trouble." Gungu was amazed. "You want trouble? No one wants that!" he said. Alur replied, "But I am curious! Please, Gungu, give me some of this trouble you've spoken of." Gungu frowned, but he said to Alur, "If you insist, I will present you with a little trouble. Send your children here tomorrow afternoon to get some trouble for you."

The next day Gungu put a hummingbird in a box and wrapped it up. When Alur's children arrived, Gungu said, "Take this present to your father. It is the trouble he asked for." The children had never heard of trouble either. As they walked home, they became curious about the contents of the box. They began to quarrel about whether they should open it. "I'll settle this!" said one child. He opened the box, and the hummingbird escaped. Now the children began to argue about whose fault it was that the bird had gotten away. When Alur came along to find his children, they were fighting and yelling.

Alur ran to Gungu's house and shouted, "What is this you have done, Gungu? My children never fought before!" Gungu replied, "Now you know what trouble is. And I hope you know something else now, too. Never think that something is wonderful just because you don't have it."

11   How did Alur feel before he visited Gungu and asked for trouble?

F   happy and content

G   nervous and unhappy

H   poor and upset

J   overwhelmed with four children

Hint: Read the first paragraph.

12   Describe how Alur felt at the end of the story.

_____

_____

_____

_____

_____

_____

Hint: Read what Alur says to Gungu.

GO ON ➤

Answers
11 Ⓕ Ⓖ Ⓗ Ⓙ

Sometimes you need to generalize. This means to come up with a general statement about something in the text.

In the 1860s, two crews set out to build a railroad. It would cross the western United States. One crew started laying tracks in Nebraska. The other crew began its work in California. Building the railroad took four years. The two crews met at Promontory Point, Utah, in May 1869. A golden spike was driven into the ground. The spike honored the completion of the railroad.

13 **From this passage, you can make the generalization that —**

   A the railroad crossed western Canada.

   B the two crews worked in directions toward each other.

   C the golden spike was driven in Nebraska.

   D Promontory Point is in California.

Hint: Cross out the choices that can be proved untrue.

TEST TIP

Trick answers often contain just one incorrect word. Be an alert reader to avoid falling for this type of error. For example, in question 13, answer A sounds reasonable except that the country named is incorrect. The answer mentions Canada while the passage talks about the United States.

The Ghost Dance is a traditional dance among many Native American tribes. Legend claims that the dance was begun by a Paiute named Wovoka, who had spoken to the Great Spirit. The Great Spirit advised the Paiute people to be good and to live in peace. He presented Wovoka with the dance and told him that if the tribe danced for five nights, they would gain happiness. He also told him that the spirits of the dead would join the tribe.

14 **Why was the Ghost Dance performed?**

_____

_____

_____

_____

_____

Hint: You need to read the entire paragraph.

STOP

Answers
13 Ⓐ Ⓑ Ⓒ Ⓓ

It is important to know the difference between fact and opinion. A fact is real and true. An opinion is a feeling or belief. Words that describe feelings or beliefs are used to offer opinions.

The wood for baseball bats comes from the ash tree forests of Pennsylvania. Ash wood is especially strong, so it makes good baseball bats. Ash trees are thin compared with other trees. In a high wind, an ash tree can break and fall. However, in the Pennsylvania forests, thicker kinds of trees grow all around the ash trees. These thick trees keep the ash trees from bending too far in a windstorm. Only a strong wooden bat can make a solid crack when it comes into contact with a baseball — and the fans love it!

1 **Which of the following is a FACT from the passage?**

    A Ash trees are the most beautiful trees.

    B Ash trees break in high winds.

    C The Pennsylvania forests have the best trees.

    D Baseball is the best sport for major league fans.

Hint: A fact is real and true.

The English word *robot* comes from another language. The Latin word *robota* means work that is dull because it has to be done over and over. This type of work is perfect for robots. Many robots are used in factories to do jobs that are hard or dangerous for people to do. They can be used to paint car parts and drill holes, make plastic food containers, and wrap ice cream bars.

2 **Which of the following is an OPINION?**

    F It is better for robots to do dull jobs than for people to do them.

    G Robots can do jobs that are dangerous.

    H The study of robots is called robotics.

    J Painting and making plastic containers are jobs that robots can do.

Hint: A fact is real and true. What is actually said in the passage? Words such as "it is better" are opinion words.

Ocean waves pound against the shore. Each wave leaves behind thousands of grains of sand. The grains of sand were once part of solid rocks. The rocks were worn down by water and weather into small grains. The wind blows the dry grains of sand into each other and into other objects. Over time the grains are molded into tiny balls. They keep this round shape for millions of years.

3 **Which of the following is an OPINION?**

    A Sand comes from rocks.

    B Water and weather wear rocks down.

    C Grains of sand stay round for millions of years.

    D It is good to have ocean waves so that we have shorelines.

Hint: Opinions describe feelings.

GO ON

Answers
1 Ⓐ Ⓑ Ⓒ Ⓓ   **2** Ⓕ Ⓖ Ⓗ Ⓙ   **3** Ⓐ Ⓑ Ⓒ Ⓓ

Horses are specially trained to do stunts in movies. You have probably seen horses fall through walls, glass windows, or even barbed-wire fences. There is no need to worry about the horses. Moviemakers use special props for such stunts. The walls are made of soft wood. The wire in the fences is really rubber. And the glass in the windows is made from sugar. This is one reason that making movies is so expensive. Most special props can be used only once, and then new ones have to be built.

4   Which of the following is an OPINION?

F   Only the best breeds of horses are used to do stunts in movies.

G   Special props are used by moviemakers to do stunts.

H   One of the high costs of making movies is special props.

J   New props are usually built after the old ones have been used only once.

Hint: An opinion is a feeling or belief.

TEST TIP

Look for signal words that make a statement an opinion. Opinions often contain exaggerations, such as *most exciting* or *least interesting*. An opinion often names something as the *best* or *worst* or claims that one thing is *better* or *worse* than another.

The American Humane Association protects horses used in making movies. Members of the group stay on movie sets to see that the horses are taken care of properly and not mistreated. The horses are protected from being hurt during exciting scenes. Have you ever seen a horse run at a full gallop for miles and miles in a movie? The horse really ran for shorter distances and was filmed each time. When the film is shown, it looks as though the horse ran a long distance. If guns are fired in a scene, the horse may have cotton in its ears for protection.

5   Which of the following is a FACT from the passage?

A   Horses make movies more exciting.

B   Horses run for miles at full gallop in order to be filmed.

C   Horses put cotton in their ears before firing guns.

D   Members of the American Humane Association protect horses.

Hint: A fact is something real and true.

STOP

Directions: Read each selection carefully. Then read each question. Darken the circle for the correct answer, or write the answers in the space provided.

| TRY THIS | More than one answer choice may seem correct. Choose the answer that goes best with the selection. |

Sample A   The Lost Dog

Mike and his father found a dog in the park. They brought it home. Mike placed an advertisement in the newspaper about finding the dog. Two days later the dog's owner came to get her dog.

How did the dog's owner find out that her dog was with Mike?

A She saw Mike with the dog.

B She read about it in the newspaper.

C Mike's father told her.

D She searched until she found her dog.

| THINK IT THROUGH | The correct answer is <u>B</u>. The third sentence tells you that Mike placed an advertisement in the newspaper. You can guess that the owner read about her dog. |

STOP

An Ancient Wonder

The Egyptians made statues of sphinxes to honor kings and queens. A sphinx has the head of a human and the body of a lion. The oldest and largest sphinx is the Great Sphinx. It was built in the desert near Giza, Egypt, thousands of years ago. At times the Great Sphinx has been buried by sand. Weather has worn away part of the stone. Today scientists are working on ways to save the Great Sphinx.

1 **What is the land like where the Great Sphinx stands?**

A snowy

B dry

C rainy

D full of trees

2 **What is a sphinx?**

_____

_____

_____

_____

_____

_____

GO ON

Answers
SA Ⓐ Ⓑ Ⓒ Ⓓ   **1** Ⓐ Ⓑ Ⓒ Ⓓ

Camino and Mr. Mishima

Mr. Mishima has a true best friend. His name is Camino, and he is a dog. Camino always helped Mr. Mishima, but one day he saved his owner's life.

Mr. Mishima was about seventy years old. He lived all alone on a farm outside of town. Most people didn't know him well. He liked to be alone, and people thought he was unfriendly. He was very strong and worked very hard to grow and harvest his crops. He grew the largest tomatoes in the county. During a very busy season, he would hire me after school to help around the farm. He always told me that I was the son he never had. Camino helped, too. Mr. Mishima loved his pet.

One day Mr. Mishima decided he would start loading the truck before I got to the farm. Sometimes he was stubborn that way. He tried lifting a very heavy crate. He felt a sharp pain in his chest and fell to the ground. Camino ran to the gas station near the farm and barked. Rubén, the gas station worker, thought the dog had gone wild. The dog began pulling and biting at Rubén's pants. Camino then ran to Rubén's jeep and leaped into the back seat. Rubén finally understood that something was wrong. He drove back to the farm and found Mr. Mishima on the ground. Rubén immediately took Mr. Mishima to the hospital.

Mr. Mishima was lucky. He had suffered a heart attack, but thanks to Camino and Rubén, he would be all right.

After Mr. Mishima had fully *recuperated*, he had a big party and invited the entire town. Everyone came to honor Camino and Rubén. But something else happened at the party, too. People finally realized that Mr. Mishima was not unfriendly after all.

GO ON

3 From the story you can assume that the author—

F thinks that Mr. Mishima should be more friendly.

G thinks that Mr. Mishima should retire.

H is fond of Mr. Mishima.

J does not like farm work.

4 If the author added a sentence to the end of the fourth paragraph, which of the following would fit best?

A I hope to work on Mr. Mishima's farm this summer, too.

B Mr. Mishima learned how to farm from his father.

C Mr. Mishima was able to return to farm work within a few weeks.

D I am able to lift the heavy crates of tomatoes.

5 Why did Camino leap into the jeep?

F He wanted Rubén to go with him to the farm.

G He wanted to go for a ride.

H He was crazy.

J He was trying to get away from Rubén.

6 In this selection, the word "recuperated" probably means—

A recovered.

B made a profit.

C doing things one's own way.

D leave.

7 How many sons did Mr. Mishima have?

F one

G two

H none

J This information is not stated in the selection.

8 Who is the author of this story?

A Mr. Mishima's son

B Camino's owner

C Rubén

D someone who works for Mr. Mishima

9 Why was Camino a special dog?

F He was excellent at farm work.

G He saved his owner's life.

H He liked to ride in automobiles.

J He knew how to do many tricks.

10 Why was Mr. Mishima lucky?

_____

_____

_____

_____

_____

_____

TEST TIP

When you are filling in the circles on standardized tests, darken the circle completely. These tests are often scored by computers. The computer must be able to read your answers clearly.

GO ON

GO ON

Answers

3 Ⓕ Ⓖ Ⓗ Ⓙ   5 Ⓕ Ⓖ Ⓗ Ⓙ   7 Ⓕ Ⓖ Ⓗ Ⓙ   9 Ⓕ Ⓖ Ⓗ Ⓙ

4 Ⓐ Ⓑ Ⓒ Ⓓ   6 Ⓐ Ⓑ Ⓒ Ⓓ   8 Ⓐ Ⓑ Ⓒ Ⓓ

Reggie Learns a Lesson

Once there was a terrible fire in a forest. The only way for a group of monkeys to survive was to escape into a river. The river had a fast current that swept the monkeys downstream. After several minutes all the monkeys were able to grab hold of a large branch. They floated on the branch for hours. The monkeys fell asleep from exhaustion. When they awoke, they found themselves *marooned* on the shore of an island.

The monkeys investigated the island and found that there were plenty of trees and generous amounts of food to eat. All the monkeys came to accept their new home, except one named Reggie. Reggie missed his old environment. He wanted to go back, but there was no way to do that.

As time passed, Reggie became lazy. He spent his days napping in the shade. The other monkeys would try to get Reggie to play with them.

"Reggie, come swing in the trees with us. Exercise. You'll feel better," they would shout to Reggie.

"Why should I? Life is uninteresting. Especially being stranded on this island. Just leave me alone. I'm tired. I'm also young. I have the rest of my life to do those kinds of things. Maybe I'll feel like doing that tomorrow," would be his reply.

One day while Reggie was napping, a trapper came to the island to capture animals for his small zoo in a nearby country. The other monkeys saw the trapper and warned Reggie. Reggie got up to run away, but he had grown fat and slow. The trapper easily imprisoned Reggie in a net. The other monkeys were strong and healthy and had no problem running away and climbing trees to escape capture.

---

11 What is meant by the word "marooned" in the first paragraph?

_____

_____

_____

_____

_____

12 Which of these proverbs best fits this selection?

A Enjoy life as it is today; tomorrow may never come.

B A penny saved is a penny earned.

C If at first you don't succeed, try, try again.

D A stitch in time saves nine.

13 This story most likely would be found in a book of—

F fables.

G facts.

H biographies.

J myths.

14 According to the selection, which of these events happened last?

A The monkeys were in a forest fire.

B The monkeys were stranded on an island.

C Reggie was captured by an animal trapper.

D Reggie napped in the shade.

GO ON

Cats: Past to Present

Cats are so popular today that about 58 million of them are kept as pets in the United States alone. Even thousands of years ago, in ancient Egypt, cats were admired and loved.

The Egyptians began to tame wild cats around 3500 B.C. These cats protected the Egyptians' crops from mice, rats, and snakes. Thus they became pets.

Greek and Phoenician traders probably brought cats to Europe and the Middle East around 1000 B.C. From the Middle East, cats spread throughout Asia. There, cats protected silkworms and temple manuscripts from rats, so they were pampered and admired.

However, cats did not do so well in Europe during the Middle Ages (A.D. 400-1500). At that time, many people believed that cats were evil, and people killed thousands of cats. Some historians believe that the destruction of so many cats led to the spread of bubonic plague, called the Black Death. This disease was spread by rats, which were no longer being killed off by cats.

By the 1600s, cats were once again popular in Europe, and explorers brought them to America. Here, they have become one of the best-loved of household pets.

15 **Which of the following expresses an opinion stated in the selection?**

F   Traders brought cats to Europe.

G   Cats are evil.

H   Cats became pets in ancient Egypt.

J   Cats were tamed by the Egyptians.

16 **When did cats come to Asia?**

_____

_____

_____

_____

17 **The selection is *mainly* about—**

A   how cats attack rats.

B   cats in ancient Egypt.

C   how cats came to America.

D   the history of cats.

18 **Cats in the Ancient Middle East and in Asia can be compared to today's—**

F   explorers.

G   security guards.

H   lions.

J   historians.

GO ON

Answers
15 Ⓕ Ⓖ Ⓗ Ⓙ   **17** Ⓐ Ⓑ Ⓒ Ⓓ   **18** Ⓕ Ⓖ Ⓗ Ⓙ

Kites Through the Ages

The oldest form of aircraft is the kite. However, no one knows where kites were first flown. Some people think the people of the South Sea Islands invented them. The people of the Solomon Islands still use kites to help with fishing. From their canoes, they fly a kite with a fishing line hanging from it. When the person in the canoe sees the line move, he or she pulls in the fish.

Some people think the art of flying kites spread to New Zealand next. The native people of New Zealand, the Maori, often made kites in the shapes of birds. They believed that birds carried messages from Earth to the gods. Some kites were designed with the bodies of birds and the heads of people. Feathers and shells were used to decorate these kites.

Most people think that the Chinese were the first to use kites. There is a story about a Chinese general who fought a battle in the year 202 B.C.

His army was surrounded by the enemy. He had his men build many kites. He told them to put a small piece of bamboo on each kite. Then he instructed the men to fly the kites over the enemy camp at night. When the wind whistled through the bamboo, the kites *shrieked*. The enemy feared they were being chased by evil spirits, and they ran away.

There is also a story about a famous Japanese thief who used a kite to reach the top of a castle. On the roof of the castle were statues of dolphins made of gold. The thief stole some of the gold from the dolphins. Then he used the kite to lower himself to the ground. Unfortunately for him, he was caught and put to death for stealing.

Kites have had many uses. In the past they have been used in scientific experiments. The National Weather Service used kites to measure the weather. Kites were also important to the development of the airplane.

Today kites are used mostly for recreation. Since the 1970s there has been renewed interest in kites. Kites come in many shapes, sizes, and colors. Kites can be flown and enjoyed the year round. There are even kite clubs and festivals in many parts of the world.

GO ON

19 In order to answer question 20, the best thing to do is—

A reread the second question.

B reread the third paragraph.

C think about the selection's mood.

D reread the entire selection.

20 The author included the third paragraph in order to—

F describe the setting of the selection.

G describe the actions of a character in the selection.

H explain the likely origin of the kite.

J summarize the main ideas in the selection.

21 Who were probably the first people to use kites?

_____

_____

_____

_____

_____

_____

22 According to the selection, in what country did a thief use a kite to steal gold?

A China

B the Solomon Islands

C India

D Japan

23 Where were kites invented?

F No one knows for sure.

G in New Zealand

H in Japan

J in China

24 According to the selection, the kite is the oldest form of—

A toy.

B aircraft.

C communication.

D art.

25 The Chinese general told his men to attach bamboo to the kites in order to—

F balance the kites.

G make the kites look better.

H make the kites shriek.

J make the kites fly higher.

26 Why did the Maori fashion kites in the shapes of birds?

A In their culture, the Maori worshipped birds as gods.

B They believed the bird shapes would make the kites fly high.

C The Maori feared birds and made the kites in bird shapes for protection from the birds.

D They believed that birds carried messages from the Maori to their gods.

27 According to the selection, kites were important to the development of the—

F yo-yo.

G submarine.

H airplane.

J gondola.

28 In line 4 of the fourth paragraph, the word "shrieked" means—

A fished.

B surrounded.

C screamed.

D fled.

GO ON ⇒

Answers

19 Ⓐ Ⓑ Ⓒ Ⓓ	**22** Ⓐ Ⓑ Ⓒ Ⓓ	**24** Ⓐ Ⓑ Ⓒ Ⓓ	**26** Ⓐ Ⓑ Ⓒ Ⓓ	**28** Ⓐ Ⓑ Ⓒ Ⓓ
20 Ⓕ Ⓖ Ⓗ Ⓙ	**23** Ⓕ Ⓖ Ⓗ Ⓙ	**25** Ⓕ Ⓖ Ⓗ Ⓙ	**27** Ⓕ Ⓖ Ⓗ Ⓙ	

An Amazing Trick

I learned a magic trick that will amaze people young and old. You will need the following supplies: a strip of paper about two inches wide by eight inches long, two paper clips, and a rubber band. Follow the steps and refer to the pictures to help you. The pictures are numbered according to the steps.

First, bring one end of the paper to the middle. Secure it with a paper clip.

Second, slip the rubber band through to the middle of the paper.

Next, bring the other end of the paper around to the front to form a loop around the first paper clip and the rubber band. Hold the middle and the front of the paper together with the second paper clip.

Fourth, say the word "Abracadabra." At the same time, pull the ends of the paper in opposite directions.

The result of the trick should be that the two clips will hang together from the rubber band on the paper.

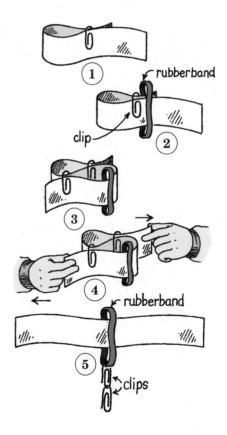

29 **If the trick is done correctly, what should happen when the ends of the strip of paper are pulled in opposite directions?**

   F The paper should rip.

   G The two paper clips should hang together from the rubber band on the paper.

   H The rubber band should stay on the paper, but the paper clips should fly off.

   J The rubber band should fly into the air, and the paper clips should remain on the paper.

30 **What should you do just before you use the strip of paper to form a loop around the first paper clip and the rubber band?**

   _____

   _____

   _____

   _____

   _____

   _____

   _____

31 **The best title for this magic trick might be—**

   A "The Amazing Clip Link."

   B "Loop de Loop."

   C "Shooting Rubber Bands."

   D "The Disappearing Paper Clips."

STOP

Answers
29 Ⓕ Ⓖ Ⓗ Ⓙ   **31** Ⓐ Ⓑ Ⓒ Ⓓ

A sample question helps you to understand the type of question you will be asked in the test that follows.

Sample A   **Buying a Reed**

Riley needed a new reed for his clarinet. He asked his teacher if he could purchase one from her. She replied, "Yes, you can buy one from me in the band room after school today."

What did Riley have to do in order to get a new reed for his clarinet?

A buy one from a music store after school

B borrow one from a band member

C buy one in the office during lunch time

D buy one in the band room after school

For questions 1–32 carefully read each selection and the questions that follow. Then darken the circle for the correct answer, or write the answer in the space provided.

A Neighborhood Ball Game

The children on Wisconsin Avenue played wiffle ball every day during the summer. One day they decided to hold a wiffle ball game to raise money to buy bats and balls. They passed out fliers to all the homes on the block. The fliers read:

> **Wiffle Ball Game**
>
> The Mighty Mites vs. The Fabulous Five
> When: Saturday, August 15
> Where: 721 S. Wisconsin
> Time: 6:00 P.M.
> Cost: Tickets $0.25 each or 5 for $1.00.
>
> Tickets are refundable if game is rained out.
>
> There will be a home-run hitting contest. The winner will receive an autographed baseball card.

1 **What was the prize for the contest?**

A a bat and ball

B a ticket to a ball game

C an autographed baseball card

D a baseball cap

2 **What would happen if it rained at game time?**

F The game would be played.

G The game would be played later.

H The game would be cancelled.

J Ticket money would be returned.

3 **Why did the children hold the game?**

_____

_____

_____

_____

_____

_____

GO ON

Answers

SA Ⓐ Ⓑ Ⓒ Ⓓ   1 Ⓐ Ⓑ Ⓒ Ⓓ   2 Ⓕ Ⓖ Ⓗ Ⓙ

A Great Woman

Marian Anderson was born in 1902 in Philadelphia. At the age of six, she was singing solos in front of the *congregation* of the Union Baptist Church. Her pure, soaring voice moved the audience, and everyone who heard her knew that the child had great talent.

Marian loved to sing. She hoped that she would be able to take singing lessons one day. But Marian's family was poor. When her father died, the family was overwhelmed with sadness and financial problems. Marian offered to quit school and go to work, but her mother refused to listen. She wanted her children to get an education.

The members of Marian's church started a collection and suggested that Marian perform at various events and make money from her singing. Marian was proud to be able to make enough money to help her family.

Marian even managed to save enough money for singing lessons. But when the music school refused to accept her because she was African-American, Marian was deeply hurt. Her mother continued to encourage her, and Marian decided to take private lessons. She had an appointment to sing for the well-known teacher Giuseppe Boghetti, who was very impressed. He said that after studying with him, Marian would be able to sing for kings and queens!

Mr. Boghetti taught Marian to sing opera. In 1925 he encouraged her to enter a contest. Although there were three hundred people entered in the contest, Marian won. She became a guest soloist with the New York Philharmonic Symphony Orchestra. She finally felt confident enough to sing anywhere. However, when Marian tried to sing at the best concert halls in the country, she was turned away because she was African-American.

Frustrated, Marian decided to go to Europe, where she hoped to be judged on her talent and not her race. During the two years she spent in Europe, Marian was made to feel very welcome. She won the admiration of Europeans in city after city. The famous conductor Arturo Toscanini told her, "A voice like yours is heard only once in a hundred years."

The overwhelming *acclamation* Marian received in Europe made new opportunities available to her in the United States. Following her return from Europe, she became the first African-American to be named a permanent member of the Metropolitan Opera Company. She also became the first African-American to perform at the White House. Through her perseverance and positive attitude, Marian Anderson was able to make the most of her talent and to open the door for other African-American performers.

GO ON ➡

4 When the author states, "Through her perseverance and positive attitude, Marian Anderson was able to make the most of her talent and to open the door for other African-American performers," the author is trying to convince the reader that—

A Marian succeeded only because her talent was so great.

B Marian's hard work and talent enabled her and others to break through the barriers of prejudice.

C Marian was only interested in making money and in furthering her own career.

D Marian probably would have been more successful if she had stayed in Europe.

5 Why did Marian offer to quit school?

_____

_____

_____

_____

_____

6 To find out more about Marian Anderson you could look in the library under—

F Famous Europeans.

G Famous Opera Singers.

H Jazz Musicians.

J History of Art.

7 The author uses the word "acclamation" in line 1 of the last paragraph to mean—

A enthusiastic approval.

B singing appearances.

C salary.

D audiences.

8 Which of these is a fact stated in the selection?

F Marian Anderson sang duets with her mother.

G Marian felt lonely in Europe.

H Marian was very close to her father.

J The members of Marian's church helped her family.

9 In line 3 of the first paragraph, the word "congregation" means—

A fire.

B assembly.

C piano.

D stage.

10 Where was Marian Anderson born and raised?

F in New York

G in Europe

H in Boston

J in Philadelphia

11 What generalization can you make about the 1920s from this selection?

A Laws ensured equal rights for all citizens.

B There was less prejudice against African-Americans at that time than there is now.

C There was more prejudice against African-Americans in the United States than in Europe.

D African-Americans had more civil rights during the 1920s than they have today.

Answers

4 (A) (B) (C) (D)   7 (A) (B) (C) (D)   9 (A) (B) (C) (D)   11 (A) (B) (C) (D)

6 (F) (G) (H) (J)   8 (F) (G) (H) (J)   10 (F) (G) (H) (J)

A Tasty Mexican Treat

Tacos are among the most popular of all Mexican foods. They are easy and fun to make, and you can vary the ingredients depending upon your taste. For example, you can use hamburger or chicken for the meat. Some people even substitute shrimp for the hamburger. You can also add hot peppers, if your mouth can take the heat!

Tacos

Ingredients:

1 box taco shells

$\frac{1}{4}$ cup oil

1 onion, chopped

1 pound hamburger (or chicken)

1 pinch cumin

1 tomato, diced

1 cup lettuce

$\frac{1}{2}$ cup cheese, grated

Hot sauce to taste

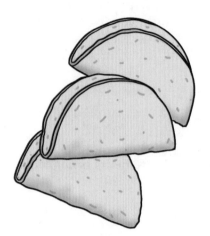

Prepare the tomato, lettuce, and cheese. Set them aside. Next, in a large pan, heat the oil and brown the onions. Add the hamburger or chicken to the onions. Stir over medium heat until the meat is browned. Add a pinch of cumin. Heat the taco shells according to the package directions. Fill the taco shells with meat, tomato, lettuce, cheese, and hot sauce. Serve with plenty of napkins!

GO ON

12 Which meat can you use instead of hamburger?

_____

_____

_____

_____

_____

13 According to the recipe for tacos, how much cumin should you use?

F $\frac{1}{3}$ cup

G 1 cup

H a pinch

J 1 teaspoon

14 Which of these ingredients is *not* cooked?

A onion

B hamburger

C tomato

D oil

15 If you wanted to learn more about Mexican food, you should—

F locate Mexico on a map.

G ask a bookstore owner.

H read a book about Mexican cooking.

J study the history of Mexico.

16 The boxes show some directions for making tacos.

Heat the oil.		Add the hamburger.
1	2	3

Which of these belongs in Box 2?

A Add cumin to meat.

B Prepare the tomato, lettuce, and cheese.

C Brown the onions.

D Fill the taco shells with the ingredients.

17 How are the taco shells prepared?

F The shells are heated in oil.

G The shells are browned with the onions.

H This information is not stated in the selection.

J They are heated according to the package directions.

18 What is the last ingredient that is put into the taco shell?

A meat

B hot sauce

C cheese

D lettuce

19 The tacos are served with napkins because they—

F are filling.

G are messy.

H are hot.

J should be carried outside.

GO ON

Answers

13 Ⓕ Ⓖ Ⓗ Ⓙ   **15** Ⓕ Ⓖ Ⓗ Ⓙ   **17** Ⓕ Ⓖ Ⓗ Ⓙ   **19** Ⓕ Ⓖ Ⓗ Ⓙ

14 Ⓐ Ⓑ Ⓒ Ⓓ   **16** Ⓐ Ⓑ Ⓒ Ⓓ   **18** Ⓐ Ⓑ Ⓒ Ⓓ

The California Gold Rush of 1848

The California Gold Rush of 1848 began at John Sutter's sawmill in the Sacramento Valley. Sutter was a shopkeeper from Switzerland. He had come to California ten years before, hoping to find a new life. He probably never dreamed that gold would be found on his land.

One day one of Mr. Sutter's partners, John Marshall, found a shiny nugget in a ditch near the sawmill. It was the size of a dime. Marshall tested the nugget to see if it was in fact the precious metal, gold. He tried shattering it and tarnishing it. He put it in lye to see if it would melt or crack. It did none of these things. Marshall was very excited and rode all one night to show the nugget to Sutter. Sutter was *skeptical* at first. He couldn't believe that there might be gold on his land. Then he tried the ultimate test. He poured nitric acid on the metal to see if it would be eaten away. It was not.

When news of the discovery broke, California was changed forever. Sutter and Marshall could no longer operate the sawmill. Their workers abandoned their jobs to search for gold. People from all over the country came to California. Even people from Europe and China arrived in California to look for gold.

New trails were opened to the West. People seemed not to mind the hardships of pioneer living as long as they found gold. In 1848 the population of California grew from 20,000 to 107,000 people. San Francisco and Sacramento were transformed from sleepy towns into booming cities. Miners who found gold were eager to spend their money in the cities. Others who were not so lucky remained in the area and became farmers or ranchers. The Gold Rush lasted from 1848 until 1852. During that time the population continued to grow, and in 1850 California became a state.

Unfortunately, the Gold Rush was not very good for Sutter and Marshall. So many people were living on the land around the sawmill that Sutter was forced to give up his claim to the land. Marshall tried searching for gold but never had much luck after that first find.

GO ON

20 This selection is *mainly* about—

  A John Sutter's sawmill.

  B early California history.

  C the life of James Marshall.

  D the Gold Rush.

21 Which of the following events happened *first?*

  F The population of California grew.

  G Marshall discovered gold near the sawmill.

  H New trails were opened to the West.

  J California became a state.

22 In line 6 of the second paragraph, the author uses the word "skeptical" to mean—

  A doubtful.

  B hopeful.

  C inspired.

  D puzzled.

23 Which word best describes California during the Gold Rush?

  F uneventful

  G pessimistic

  H prosperous

  J frightening

24 Why did so many people leave their homes and jobs to search for gold?

_____

_____

_____

_____

_____

25 According to the selection, why is gold considered a precious metal?

  A It is easily tarnished, and lye melts it.

  B It is very valuable.

  C People use it to make chains and other jewelry.

  D It is used only to make coins.

26 What are paragraphs 3 and 4 *mainly* about?

  F how California became a state

  G how the Gold Rush affected California

  H how people lived in California during the Gold Rush

  J how gold was discovered in California

27 The author included the first paragraph in order to—

  A introduce an important character.

  B describe the setting.

  C describe the mood.

  D explain the term "Gold Rush."

28 Why did the author write this selection?

_____

_____

_____

_____

_____

_____

_____

Frontier Adventure

The February wind blew chill across the prairie. Mae and Milly huddled together in the wagon, trying to stay warm. Soon their father would stop to make camp for the night. Then they could build a fire to warm themselves. The sisters watched their mother. She was swaying with the motion of the wagon as she mended their clothes. When they reached their new home on the frontier, there would be no store nearby to buy things. They would have to make do with what they had. That seemed both scary and exciting to the girls. This move was really an adventure.

Suddenly the girls heard their father shout, "Quick, come up here and look at this!" The girls and their mother crawled to the front of the wagon, opened the flap, and looked out upon a large herd of buffalo. The powerful animals with their brown, shaggy coats moved slowly toward the south. They kept their backs to the wind, which seemed to blow colder as the day progressed.

"This might be a good stopping place. It looks like we might be in for some bad weather," their father said. Clouds were gathering on the northern horizon as the family prepared for the night. Mae helped her father look for dry brush to start a fire, while Milly and her mother made preparations for dinner. They all worked quickly, sensing that they had a long night ahead.

29 Why was the family expecting a long, hard night?

_____

_____

_____

_____

_____

30 The family was traveling in—

F a canoe.

G a railroad compartment.

H a covered wagon.

J a houseboat.

31 There is enough information in this selection to learn how—

A to mend clothes.

B pioneers traveled across the prairie.

C to make camp.

D buffalo crossed the prairie.

32 According to the selection, how many family members are making the journey?

F three

G four

H five

J seven

STOP

Answers
30 (F) (G) (H) (J)   **31** (A) (B) (C) (D)   **32** (F) (G) (H) (J)

READING VOCABULARY

─IDENTIFYING WORD MEANINGS─

Directions: Darken the circle for the word or group of words that has the same or almost the same meaning as the underlined word, or write in the answer.

TRY THIS | Choose your answer carefully. The other choices may seem correct. Be sure to think about the meaning of the underlined word.

Sample A

To <u>chat</u> is to—

A agree   C plan

B laugh   D talk

 THINK IT THROUGH | The correct answer is <u>D</u>. To <u>chat</u> is to <u>talk</u>. To <u>chat</u> is not to agree, laugh, or plan.

STOP

---

1 A <u>drill</u> is—

A an engine   C a fire

B an exit   D an exercise

2 Something that is <u>brief</u> is—

F long   H serious

G thin   J short

3 To <u>admit</u> something is to—

A hide it   C improve it

B confess it   D change it

4 A person who is <u>idle</u> is—

F busy   H loyal

G lazy   J quick

5 A <u>festival</u> is a kind of—

A journey   C song

B celebration   D dessert

6 Something that is <u>urgent</u> is—

F confusing   H important

G silly   J simple

7 A walk that is <u>brisk</u> is—

A slow   C fun

B quick   D steady

8 If you are <u>chilly</u>, you are—

_____

_____

_____

_____

STOP

Answers

SA Ⓐ Ⓑ Ⓒ Ⓓ   2 Ⓕ Ⓖ Ⓗ Ⓙ   4 Ⓕ Ⓖ Ⓗ Ⓙ   6 Ⓕ Ⓖ Ⓗ Ⓙ

1 Ⓐ Ⓑ Ⓒ Ⓓ   3 Ⓐ Ⓑ Ⓒ Ⓓ   5 Ⓐ Ⓑ Ⓒ Ⓓ   7 Ⓐ Ⓑ Ⓒ Ⓓ

Directions: Darken the circle for the sentence in which the underlined word means the same as it does in the sentence in the box.

 TRY THIS — Read the sentence in the box carefully. Decide what the underlined word means. Then look for the sentence in which the underlined word has the same meaning.

Sample A

> We saw the deer easily <u>clear</u> the fence.

In which sentence does <u>clear</u> have the same meaning as it does in the sentence above?

A Will that runner <u>clear</u> the hurdle?

B I need to <u>clear</u> this issue with the boss.

C It was a crisp, <u>clear</u> morning.

D Her speech was loud and <u>clear</u>.

THINK IT THROUGH — The correct answer is A. In this sentence and in the sentence in the box, <u>clear</u> means "to pass without touching."

 STOP

---

1   > Miranda seems to <u>favor</u> the color purple.

In which sentence does <u>favor</u> have the same meaning as it does in the sentence above?

A I will do this as a <u>favor</u>.

B She has a puzzle as a party <u>favor</u>.

C The people <u>favor</u> keeping that law.

D Does the baby <u>favor</u> his mother?

2   > Judy placed a <u>fork</u> on the table.

In which sentence does <u>fork</u> have the same meaning as it does in the sentence above?

F Turn right at the <u>fork</u> in the road.

G The child is learning to eat with a <u>fork</u>.

H Jake used a tuning <u>fork</u> to fix the piano.

J Mary sat in the <u>fork</u> of the tree.

3   > First, <u>stir</u> the paint.

In which sentence does <u>stir</u> have the same meaning as it does in the sentence above?

A Ming didn't <u>stir</u> during the scary movie.

B The speech created quite a <u>stir</u>.

C You must <u>stir</u> the sauce until it thickens.

D See the wind <u>stir</u> the leaves.

4   > She didn't leave a <u>drop</u> of juice.

In which sentence does <u>drop</u> have the same meaning as it does in the sentence above?

F The price of the skates will <u>drop</u>.

G The baby was about to <u>drop</u> his toy.

H There was one <u>drop</u> of medicine left.

J Can we please <u>drop</u> the subject?

STOP

Answers
SA Ⓐ Ⓑ Ⓒ Ⓓ   1 Ⓐ Ⓑ Ⓒ Ⓓ   2 Ⓕ Ⓖ Ⓗ Ⓙ   3 Ⓐ Ⓑ Ⓒ Ⓓ   4 Ⓕ Ⓖ Ⓗ Ⓙ

Directions: Darken the circle for the word or words that give the meaning of the underlined word, or write in the answer.

> **TRY THIS**
>
> Read the first sentence carefully. Look for clue words in the sentence. Then use each answer choice in place of the underlined word. Remember that the underlined word and your answer must have the same meaning.

Sample A

Grandpa <u>recalled</u> the games he played as a child. <u>Recalled</u> means—

A remembered

B played

C forgot

D listed

> **THINK IT THROUGH**
>
> The correct answer is <u>A</u>. The clue words are "Grandpa" and "child." Grandpa would remember games he had played as a child.

---

1 The students were surprised by the principal's <u>startling</u> announcement. <u>Startling</u> means—

A unexpected

B daily

C brief

D usual

2 The <u>acute</u> ache in her side caused Minnie intense pain. <u>Acute</u> means—

F frequent

G occasional

H slight

J severe

3 Karen noticed items missing from the store's <u>inventory</u>. <u>Inventory</u> means—

A warehouse

B bill

C property

D truck

4 She didn't like the dance because it had <u>complicated</u> steps. <u>Complicated</u> means—

_____

_____

_____

_____

5 Jean has won <u>numerous</u> awards for all her paintings. <u>Numerous</u> means—

F many

G secret

H art

J foreign

6 The heavy rains <u>replenished</u> the empty well. <u>Replenished</u> means—

A refilled

B destroyed

C ruined

D poisoned

Answers

SA Ⓐ Ⓑ Ⓒ Ⓓ   2 Ⓕ Ⓖ Ⓗ Ⓙ   5 Ⓕ Ⓖ Ⓗ Ⓙ

1 Ⓐ Ⓑ Ⓒ Ⓓ   3 Ⓐ Ⓑ Ⓒ Ⓓ   6 Ⓐ Ⓑ Ⓒ Ⓓ

Sample A

To investigate is to—

A plan

B hide

C mix

D examine

STOP

For questions 1–8, darken the circle for the word or words that have the same or almost the same meaning as the underlined word.

1 Something that is incomplete is—

A finished

B excellent

C unfinished

D perfect

2 To resume is to—

F end

G begin

H hide

J continue

3 Something that is brutal is—

A harsh

B gentle

C warm

D soft

4 Someone who is courageous is—

F brave

G friendly

H shy

J afraid

5 A solution is—

A a plan

B an answer

C a question

D a trick

6 A tradition is the same as—

F a sport

G an activity

H a barrier

J a custom

7 An error is a—

A game

B race

C mistake

D visitor

8 An academy is a kind of—

F school

G family

H channel

J custom

Write your answer for the following:

9 Someone who is weary is—

_____

_____

_____

_____

_____

_____

STOP

Answers

SA Ⓐ Ⓑ Ⓒ Ⓓ	**2** Ⓕ Ⓖ Ⓗ Ⓙ	**4** Ⓕ Ⓖ Ⓗ Ⓙ	**6** Ⓕ Ⓖ Ⓗ Ⓙ	**8** Ⓕ Ⓖ Ⓗ Ⓙ	
1 Ⓐ Ⓑ Ⓒ Ⓓ	**3** Ⓐ Ⓑ Ⓒ Ⓓ	**5** Ⓐ Ⓑ Ⓒ Ⓓ	**7** Ⓐ Ⓑ Ⓒ Ⓓ		

Sample B

> Marissa tried to spare her sister's feelings.

In which sentence does spare have the same meaning as it does in the sentence above?

A   The spare tire was also flat.

B   Do you have any spare change?

C   The knight decided to spare the dragon.

D   We have a spare bedroom for guests.

STOP

For questions 10–14, darken the circle for the sentence in which the underlined word means the same as it does in the sentence in the box.

10
> The steps to our porch are not level.

In which sentence does level have the same meaning as it does in the sentence above?

A   This recipe requires one level teaspoon of sugar.

B   We traveled high above sea level.

C   Manuel advanced to the next level of tennis.

D   She used a level to make sure the shelf was straight.

11
> She scored double the points of her friend.

In which sentence does double have the same meaning as it does in the sentence above?

F   The pilot lived a double life as a spy.

G   The twin was his double.

H   Zack hit a double in today's game.

J   Six is the double of three.

12
> Ben read the instructions on the computer monitor.

In which sentence does monitor have the same meaning as it does in the sentence above?

A   Her job is to be the playground monitor.

B   A radar device will monitor the traffic.

C   The monitor recorded the patient's heartbeat.

D   Who will monitor the players?

13
> Be sure to pound the nail in carefully.

In which sentence does pound have the same meaning as it does in the sentence above?

F   Ned had to pound the tent stakes into the ground.

G   This weighs little more than one pound.

H   His heart began to pound as he stepped up to the plate.

J   They went to a pound to find a new puppy.

14
> The soccer ball rolled past the foul line.

In which sentence does foul have the same meaning as it does in the sentence above?

A   Our plane was delayed due to foul weather.

B   The chemical gave off a foul odor.

C   That group was guilty of foul play.

D   The batter hit a foul ball.

STOP

Answers

SB Ⓐ Ⓑ Ⓒ Ⓓ	11 Ⓕ Ⓖ Ⓗ Ⓙ	13 Ⓕ Ⓖ Ⓗ Ⓙ	
10 Ⓐ Ⓑ Ⓒ Ⓓ	12 Ⓐ Ⓑ Ⓒ Ⓓ	14 Ⓐ Ⓑ Ⓒ Ⓓ	

Sample C

The celebration is about to <u>commence</u>. <u>Commence</u> means to—

A begin

B end

C continue

D close

STOP

For questions 15–21, darken the circle for the word or words that give the meaning of the underlined word.

15 They set up camp in a <u>remote</u> part of the forest. <u>Remote</u> means—

F small

G large

H distant

J woody

16 The two politicians <u>collided</u> over the new tax plans. <u>Collided</u> means—

A talked favorably

B agreed to discuss

C supported

D strongly disagreed

17 Make sure to <u>secure</u> the lock on the door. <u>Secure</u> means—

F fasten

G open

H measure

J insert

18 We laughed aloud at her <u>hilarious</u> tale. <u>Hilarious</u> means—

A obviously fictional

B very stupid

C extremely funny

D quite offensive

19 Be <u>specific</u> about what you need done. <u>Specific</u> means—

F unsure

G secretive

H vague

J definite

20 She <u>indicated</u> the route to take to the store. <u>Indicated</u> means—

A closed

B drove off

C pointed out

D left

21 The fast-running river flowed <u>rapidly</u> down the steep mountainside. <u>Rapidly</u> means—

F slowly

G swiftly

H lazily

J secretly

Write your answer for the following:

22 The novel has an interesting <u>plot</u>. What is the <u>plot</u> of a novel?

_____

_____

_____

_____

STOP

Answers

SC Ⓐ Ⓑ Ⓒ Ⓓ **16** Ⓐ Ⓑ Ⓒ Ⓓ **18** Ⓐ Ⓑ Ⓒ Ⓓ **20** Ⓐ Ⓑ Ⓒ Ⓓ

15 Ⓕ Ⓖ Ⓗ Ⓙ **17** Ⓕ Ⓖ Ⓗ Ⓙ **19** Ⓕ Ⓖ Ⓗ Ⓙ **21** Ⓕ Ⓖ Ⓗ Ⓙ

MATH PROBLEM-SOLVING PLAN

OVERVIEW

THE PROBLEM-SOLVING PLAN

When solving math problems follow these steps:

STEP 1: WHAT IS THE QUESTION/GOAL?

Decide what must be found. This information is usually presented in the form of a question.

STEP 2: FIND THE FACTS

Locate the factual information in three different ways:

    A. **KEY FACTS** are the facts you need to solve the problem.

    B. **FACTS YOU DON'T NEED** are those facts that are not necessary for solving the problem.

    C. **ARE MORE FACTS NEEDED?** Decide if you have enough information to solve the problem.

STEP 3: SELECT A STRATEGY

Decide what strategies you might use, how you will use them, and then estimate what your answer will be. If one strategy doesn't help you to solve the problem, try another.

STEP 4: SOLVE

Apply the strategy according to your plan. Use an operation if necessary, and clearly indicate your answer.

STEP 5: DOES YOUR RESPONSE MAKE SENSE?

Check to make sure that your answer makes sense. Use estimation or approximation strategies.

Directions: Use the problem-solving plan to solve this math problem.

PROBLEM/QUESTION:

Mr. Gonzalez is a salesman from Manorville. He drove 45 miles to visit his first customer in Boston. The drive took him 1 hour. On his return trip he drove an extra 30 minutes to visit a customer in Oaktown, which is 15 miles north of Boston. If Manorville is west of Boston, draw a map of the trip.

STEP 1: WHAT IS THE QUESTION/GOAL?

_____

_____

_____

STEP 2: FIND THE FACTS

_____

_____

_____

STEP 3: SELECT A STRATEGY

_____

_____

_____

STEP 4: SOLVE

STEP 5: DOES YOUR RESPONSE MAKE SENSE?

_____

_____

_____

_____

Directions: Use the problem-solving plan to solve this math problem.

PROBLEM/QUESTION:

Su Ling went to the bookstore to buy 5 books. Each of the books costs $4.95. Su Ling thought the total cost for the 5 books should be about $19.50. Is Su Ling correct? If she is wrong, what mistake did she make when she figured out the price.

STEP 1: WHAT IS THE QUESTION/GOAL?

_____

_____

_____

STEP 2: FIND THE FACTS

_____

_____

_____

STEP 3: SELECT A STRATEGY

_____

_____

_____

STEP 4: SOLVE

_____

_____

_____

STEP 5: DOES YOUR RESPONSE MAKE SENSE?

_____

_____

_____

_____

MATH PROBLEM SOLVING

UNDERSTANDING NUMBER RELATIONSHIPS

Directions: Darken the circle for the correct answer, or write in the answer.

> **TRY THIS** Read each question twice before choosing your answer. Be sure to think about which numbers stand for ones, tens, hundreds, and so on.

Sample A

The triangles represent what fraction of all the shapes shown?

> **THINK IT THROUGH** The correct answer is <u>A</u>. There are a total of 7 shapes in the picture. 3 of these shapes are triangles. This is expressed as the fraction $\frac{3}{7}$.

A $\frac{3}{7}$ **C** $\frac{4}{7}$

B $\frac{3}{4}$ **D** $\frac{1}{2}$

STOP

---

1 Jim's most recent recorded times for the 100-meter dash were: 12.2 seconds, 12.09 seconds, 12.225 seconds, and 12.53 seconds. List these times from fastest to slowest.

_____

_____

_____

_____

2 Vicky needs $2\frac{1}{4}$ yards of green ribbon, $1\frac{3}{4}$ yards of pink ribbon, $\frac{7}{8}$ yards of purple ribbon, and $2\frac{1}{2}$ yards of yellow ribbon for a spring basket. Which list shows the ribbons from least amount to greatest amount?

A green, yellow, pink, purple

B yellow, purple, green, pink

C purple, pink, green, yellow

D pink, purple, yellow, green

3 The new hockey team in town set a record selling 1,216,115 tickets to their third home game. How is 1,216,115 written in words?

F twelve million sixteen thousand one hundred fifteen

G one hundred twenty-one million six thousand fifteen

H one hundred thousand twenty-one thousand one hundred fifteen

J one million two hundred sixteen thousand one hundred fifteen

4 Which fraction means the same as $\frac{9}{12}$?

A $\frac{1}{3}$ **C** $\frac{2}{3}$

B $\frac{12}{9}$ **D** $\frac{3}{4}$

5 Which of these numbers is greater than 2,510 and less than 2,901?

F 2,505 **H** 2,888

G 2,911 **J** 2,910

STOP

Answers

SA Ⓐ Ⓑ Ⓒ Ⓓ **3** Ⓕ Ⓖ Ⓗ Ⓙ **5** Ⓕ Ⓖ Ⓗ Ⓙ

2 Ⓐ Ⓑ Ⓒ Ⓓ **4** Ⓐ Ⓑ Ⓒ Ⓓ

Directions: Darken the circle for the correct answer, or write in the answer.

TRY THIS Work each problem on scratch paper. Try each answer choice in the problem before you choose your answer. Remember to think about which numbers stand for ones, tens, hundreds, and so on.

Sample A

What number is shown here in expanded form?

2,000 + 400 + 2

A 242

C 2,042

B 2,420

D 2,402

THINK IT THROUGH The correct answer is <u>D</u>. First, place the numbers in a column:

2,000
400
+   2

and then add.

STOP

---

1 In which of the following numbers does the 6 stand for 6 hundreds?

A 246

B 468

C 637

D 6,052

2 Which number has an 8 in the ten thousands place and a 1 in the hundreds place?

F 982,135

G 153,982

H 298,351

J 581,293

3 Carlos wants a group of 27 girls and 18 boys to form into teams so that each team will have an equal number of boys and an equal number of girls. What is the greatest number of teams Carlos can form?

A 9

B 6

C 3

D 2

4 Laura will pay $50 more in rent on her apartment in two months. If she is paying $640 now, what will her monthly rent be in two months?

F $590

G $645

H $690

J $1,140

5 In the numeral 246,738, which digit is in the hundreds place?

_____

_____

_____

_____

6 What is the value of the 6 in 85.26?

A 6 tenths

B 6 hundredths

C 6 thousandths

D 6 tens

STOP

Answers

SA ⒶⒷⒸⒹ   2 ⒻⒼⒽⒿ   4 ⒻⒼⒽⒿ
1 ⒶⒷⒸⒹ   3 ⒶⒷⒸⒹ   6 ⒶⒷⒸⒹ

Directions: Darken the circle for the correct answer, or write in the answer.

TRY THIS

Check your work by making sure both sides of an equation are equal values. Try using all the answer choices in the problem.

Sample A

If $25 - y = 18$, what is the value of y?

A   4

B   7

C   18

D   43

THINK IT THROUGH

The correct answer is B. Subtract 18 from both sides of the equation, and $y = 25 - 18 = \underline{7}$.

STOP

---

1 Which expression could be used to find the number of inches there are in 5 yards 1 foot?

A $(36 + 5) - 12$

B $(36 - 12) \times 12$

C $(36 + 5) \times (12 \times 1)$

D $(36 \times 5) + (12 \times 1)$

2 Which of the following problems could be solved by using the equation $60 = t + 45$?

F   Wanda bought 60 cookies on Tuesday and 45 cookies on Wednesday. How many cookies did she buy?

G   Jim practiced the piano for 45 minutes today. He tries to practice 1 hour each day. How many minutes does he still have to practice?

H   The cab driver started the day with $60 and earned $45 more. How much does he have now?

J   The souvenir shop sells shells for 60 cents each. They sold 45 shells. How much money did the shop make from the sale of the shells?

3 If $y + 13 = 25$, then $y =$

A   6   C   15

B   12   D   38

4 What number makes the number sentence true?

$6 + (3 + 5) = (6 + \square) + 5$

F   3   H   11

G   8   J   13

5 Choose the number sentence that is in the same fact family as $8 + 3 = 11$.

A $8 \times 3 = 24$ C $11 - 3 = 8$

B $5 + 6 = 11$ D $8 - 11 = 3$

6 If $x = 7$, then $x + 4 =$

_____

_____

_____

_____

STOP

Answers

SA Ⓐ Ⓑ Ⓒ Ⓓ   2 Ⓕ Ⓖ Ⓗ Ⓙ   4 Ⓕ Ⓖ Ⓗ Ⓙ

1 Ⓐ Ⓑ Ⓒ Ⓓ   3 Ⓐ Ⓑ Ⓒ Ⓓ   5 Ⓐ Ⓑ Ⓒ Ⓓ

Directions: Darken the circle for the correct answer, or write in the answer.

> **TRY THIS**
> Read each problem carefully. Study the graphs or other visual materials, and look for key words or numbers to help you choose your answer.

Sample A

In a total of 10 spins, which number will the spinner probably point to the greatest number of times?

A 1
B 2
C 4
D 5

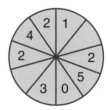

> **THINK IT THROUGH**
> The correct answer is <u>B</u>. The number <u>2</u> appears 3 times on the spinner. This is more often than any other number.

STOP

---

1 The graph shows the number of cans 3 classes collected for recycling. How many more cans did Grade 4 collect than Grade 6?

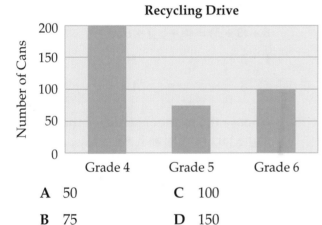

Recycling Drive

A 50   C 100

B 75   D 150

2 With his eyes closed, which card will Cal most likely pick?

D B A C A
B D B D D

F A   H C

G B   J D

3 Lola has been saving money for her summer vacation. The last four deposits she made to her savings account were $17, $22, $34, and $26. What is the average of Lola's deposits?

_____

_____

_____

_____

_____

_____

4 The sports store sells shirts with long sleeves or short sleeves. They come in small, medium, large, and extra large sizes. They are available in blue with white letters, white with blue letters, and white with red letters. How many total choices of shirts are there?

A 9 choices   C 24 choices

B 12 choices   D 48 choices

GO ON

Answers
SA Ⓐ Ⓑ Ⓒ Ⓓ   **1** Ⓐ Ⓑ Ⓒ Ⓓ   **2** Ⓕ Ⓖ Ⓗ Ⓙ   **4** Ⓐ Ⓑ Ⓒ Ⓓ

The graph shows the number of hours Lena baby-sat last week. Study the graph. Then answer questions 5–7.

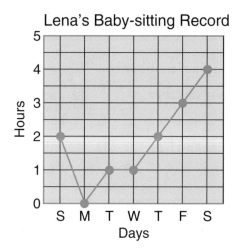

Lena's Baby-sitting Record

5 How many hours did Lena baby-sit during this week?

F 16 hours   **H** 10 hours

G 13 hours   **J** 6 hours

6 On which day did Lena baby-sit the most hours?

A Sunday   **C** Saturday

B Thursday   **D** Monday

7 On which day did Lena baby-sit for 3 hours?

F Friday   **H** Thursday

G Sunday   **J** Saturday

8 Marcus bowled 113 the first game, 124 the second game, and 132 the third game. What was his bowling average?

_____

_____

_____

_____

9 Which tally chart was used to make the bar graph?

A

Carmen	𝍬 𝍬 𝍬 I
Lizzie	𝍬 𝍬 𝍬 𝍬
Lauren	𝍬 𝍬 𝍬
Michiko	𝍬 𝍬 II

B

Carmen	𝍬 III
Lizzie	𝍬 𝍬
Lauren	𝍬 II
Michiko	𝍬 I

C

Carmen	𝍬 𝍬 II
Lizzie	𝍬 𝍬 𝍬
Lauren	𝍬 𝍬 𝍬 𝍬
Michiko	𝍬 𝍬 𝍬 I

D

Carmen	𝍬 𝍬 𝍬 IIII
Lizzie	𝍬 𝍬 II
Lauren	𝍬 𝍬 IIII
Michiko	𝍬 𝍬 I

The bar graph shows the number of butterflies collected by four students during one week.

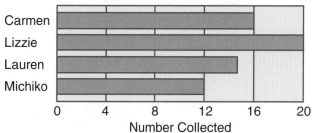

BUTTERFLY RECORD

Number Collected

10 How many more butterflies did Carmen collect than Michiko?

F 2   **H** 4

G 3   **J** 6

Answers

5 Ⓕ Ⓖ Ⓗ Ⓙ   **6** Ⓐ Ⓑ Ⓒ Ⓓ   **7** Ⓕ Ⓖ Ⓗ Ⓙ   **9** Ⓐ Ⓑ Ⓒ Ⓓ   **10** Ⓕ Ⓖ Ⓗ Ⓙ

Directions: Darken the circle for the correct answer, or write in the answer.

 TRY THIS

Read each problem carefully. Try using all the answer choices in the problem. Then choose the answer that you think best answers the question.

Sample A

A special machine multiplies any number entered into it by 6. The table shows how the numbers are changed. Which numbers are missing from the table?

Original number	5	7	10
New number	30		

A 13 and 16   C 36 and 42

B 42 and 52   D 42 and 60

THINK IT THROUGH

The correct answer is <u>D</u>. Multiply 7 × 6, which equals <u>42</u>. Next, multiply 10 × 6, which equals <u>60</u>.

STOP

---

1 Look at the pattern shown here. What number is missing from this number pattern?

101, 105, _____, 113, 117

A 107

B 110

C 109

D 112

2 Tim keeps a journal for his reading class. In it he records the number of hours and the number of pages he reads each week. Find the missing value in the table shown here.

Hours	3	6	18	36
Number of pages	40	80		480

_____

_____

_____

_____

3 Which piece of material is the one that has been cut out from the fabric?

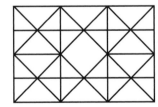

F

G

H

J

STOP

Answers
SA Ⓐ Ⓑ Ⓒ Ⓓ   **1** Ⓐ Ⓑ Ⓒ Ⓓ   **3** Ⓕ Ⓖ Ⓗ Ⓙ

Directions: Darken the circle for the correct answer, or write in the answer.

> **TRY THIS**
>
> Round numbers when you estimate. For some problems, there are no exact answers. Then you should take your best guess. You can check your answer by using the numbers given in the problem.

Sample A

During the summer Arturo swims about 42 minutes every day. A reasonable amount of time in minutes that he would swim in 2 months is—

A   100 minutes   C   240 minutes

B   80 minutes   D   2,400 minutes

> **THINK IT THROUGH**
>
> The correct answer is <u>D</u>. Start by rounding 42 to 40. There are about 60 days in 2 months. $60 \times 40 = $ <u>2,400 minutes</u>. The answer would not be 100, 80, or 240 minutes.

1   Mrs. Shriver's farm stand had 527 pumpkins. She sold 215 of them. Which is the best estimate of the number of pumpkins she has left?

A   100

B   200

C   300

D   400

2   Carmelo's Restaurant bought 32 boxes of napkins. There were 250 napkins in each box. *About* how many napkins did the restaurant buy?

_____

_____

_____

_____

_____

3   Use the table below to answer questions 3 and 4.

MENU	
Hamburger	$1.75
Hot dog	$1.25
Pizza	$2.00
Fruit	$0.50
Juice	$0.50
Milk	$0.40
Chips	$0.25

According to this menu, *about* how much does a hamburger and a carton of milk cost?

F $1.50   H $3.00

G $2.00   J $4.00

4   *About* how much change should Leon receive from $10.00 if he bought 2 hot dogs, a bag of chips, and a carton of milk?

A $3.00   C $5.00

B $4.75   D $7.00

Answers

SA Ⓐ Ⓑ Ⓒ Ⓓ   1 Ⓐ Ⓑ Ⓒ Ⓓ   3 Ⓕ Ⓖ Ⓗ Ⓙ   4 Ⓐ Ⓑ Ⓒ Ⓓ

Directions: Darken the circle for the correct answer, or write in the answer.

TRY THIS Use the objects shown to help you answer each question. Remember that perimeter is the measurement around the <u>outside</u>, while <u>area</u> is the measurement of the <u>inside</u> of a space.

Sample A

What is the area of the square shown here?

8 m

A   32 square meters

B   64 square meters

C   96 square meters

D   256 square meters

THINK IT THROUGH The correct answer is <u>B</u>. Each side of the square is 8m. To find the area, multiply 8m × 8m, which equals <u>64 square meters</u>.

STOP

Use the grid of a park shown here to answer questions 1 and 2.

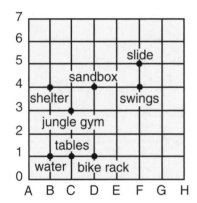

1   Which three items in the park are next to one another in a straight row?

_____

_____

_____

_____

2   More swings will be installed at F2. What will be closest to these swings?

A   slide   C   water

B   bike rack   D   other swings

3   What is the perimeter of the plot of land shown here?

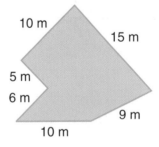

_____

_____

_____

_____

GO ON

Answers
SA Ⓐ Ⓑ Ⓒ Ⓓ   **2** Ⓐ Ⓑ Ⓒ Ⓓ

4 The perimeter of a triangle measures 30 centimeters. Two sides of the triangle measure 8 centimeters and 14 centimeters. What is the length of the third side of this triangle?

F 6 centimeters   H 14 centimeters

G 8 centimeters   J 22 centimeters

5 Which transformation moves the figure from position A to position B?

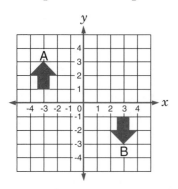

A reflection   C rotation

B slide   D translation

6 How many sides does a trapezoid have?

F 4   H 6

G 5   J 8

7 The quadrilaterals are grouped together. The other figures are not quadrilaterals.

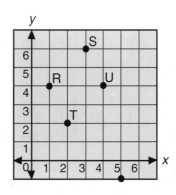

Which shape below is a quadrilateral?

A   C

B   D

8 The length of Keiko's rectangular cookie sheet is 36 centimeters, and its width is 15 centimeters. What is the perimeter of the cookie sheet?

F 540 centimeters   H 51 centimeters

G 102 centimeters   J 21 centimeters

9 Which ordered pair is best represented by point S?

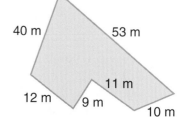

A (1, 4)   C (2, 2)

B (4, 4)   D (3, 6)

10 This is a diagram of the playground at Beth's school. What is its perimeter?

F 135 m

G 125 m

H 114 m

J 105 m

11 Which angle is a right angle?

A   C

B   D

STOP

Directions: Darken the circle for the correct answer, or write in the answer.

TRY THIS — Study the words in each problem carefully. Then decide what you have to do to find the answer.

Sample A

It was 9:00 P.M. when Sara went to bed. Which clock shows the time three and one-half hours later?

A 9:30 P.M.   C 12:30 A.M.

B 1:30 A.M.   D 12:40 A.M.

THINK IT THROUGH — The correct answer is <u>C</u>. Going ahead 3 hours from 9 P.M. moves the clock to 12 A.M. Another 30 minutes added brings the time to <u>12:30 A.M.</u>

---

1 Which metric unit of measurement is best to use to describe the height of a tree?

A kilometers

B millimeters

C liters

D meters

2 Alice put some muffins into the oven to bake at the time shown on the clock. It takes forty-five minutes for the muffins to bake. What time will the muffins be done?

3 Which of these would hold a quart when full?

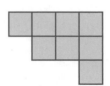

F   H

G   J

4 What is the area of this figure in square units?

= 1 square unit

A 14 square units   C 8 square units

B 12 square units   D 6 square units

GO ON

Answers

SA Ⓐ Ⓑ Ⓒ Ⓓ   1 Ⓐ Ⓑ Ⓒ Ⓓ   3 Ⓕ Ⓖ Ⓗ Ⓙ   4 Ⓐ Ⓑ Ⓒ Ⓓ

5 Which of these equals the greatest amount of liquid?

F 1 gallon

G 2 quarts

H 3 pints

J 4 cups

6 Which unit of measurement is best to use to describe the weight of a bucket of sand?

A feet

B miles

C liters

D pounds

7 Use your inch ruler and the map to help you answer the question. What is the actual distance from Camp River Trails to State Park?

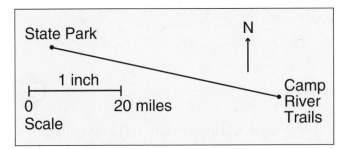

F 50 miles

G 60 miles

H 40 miles

J 45 miles

8 How many feet are there between the two trees?

27 yards

A 27 feet

B 9 feet

C 81 feet

D 972 feet

9 What is the area of this figure?

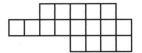

F 22 square units

G 17 square units

H 18 square units

J 12 square units

10 The length of an automobile would be best expressed in—

A centimeters.

B inches.

C feet.

D kilometers.

11 Use your centimeter ruler to answer this question.

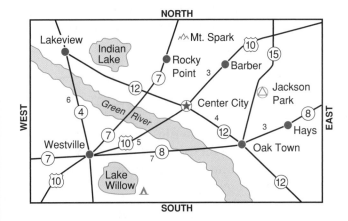

About how many centimeters longer is it from Lakeview to Oak Town on Highways 4 and 8 than on Highway 12?

_____

_____

_____

_____

STOP

Answers

5 Ⓕ Ⓖ Ⓗ Ⓙ   **7** Ⓕ Ⓖ Ⓗ Ⓙ   **9** Ⓕ Ⓖ Ⓗ Ⓙ

6 Ⓐ Ⓑ Ⓒ Ⓓ   **8** Ⓐ Ⓑ Ⓒ Ⓓ   **10** Ⓐ Ⓑ Ⓒ Ⓓ

Directions: Darken the circle for the correct answer, or write in the answer.

 TRY THIS Study the words in each problem carefully. Then decide what you have to do to find the answer.

Sample A

Henry has 50 pages in his stamp album. He needs 32 more stamps to complete his collection. What other information is needed to find the total number of stamps Henry will have in his collection?

A the number of stamps on each page

B the number of stamps he bought last week

C the cost of each stamp

D the size of each stamp

 THINK IT THROUGH The correct answer is A. The number of pages (50) in the stamp album is known. If we can find out how many stamps are on each page, we can find the total number of stamps in the completed collection.

STOP

---

1 There are 5 boxes of candles. Each box holds 25 candles. How many candles are there in all?

_____

_____

2 Juan needs some tiles similar to the one shown on the left. How many tiles like this one can he get from the large figure shown?

 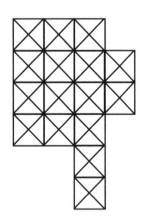

A 6
B 8
C 12
D 16

3 Brand A laundry soap costs more than Brand D laundry soap. Brand D costs less than Brand X. Brand Z costs more than Brand A. Which of the following is most reasonable?

F Brand Z costs more than Brand D.

G Brand X and Brand A cost the same.

H Brand Z costs less than Brand X.

J Brand A costs more than Brand X.

4 Which figure is made of all rectangles?

A 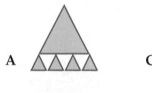 C

B D

Answers
SA Ⓐ Ⓑ Ⓒ Ⓓ   2 Ⓐ Ⓑ Ⓒ Ⓓ   3 Ⓕ Ⓖ Ⓗ Ⓙ   4 Ⓐ Ⓑ Ⓒ Ⓓ

Directions: Darken the circle for the correct answer. Darken the circle for NH (Not Here) if the correct answer is not given. If no choices are given, write in the answer.

TRY THIS

When adding columns of digits, remember to rename when necessary. Write the sum and check it against the choices.

Sample A

$$\frac{2}{3} + \frac{1}{5}$$

A $\frac{1}{8}$
B $\frac{1}{4}$
C $\frac{7}{15}$
D $\frac{13}{15}$
E NH

THINK IT THROUGH

The correct answer is D. First, find the least common denominator, which is 15. Convert each fraction to fifteenths: $\frac{2}{3} = \frac{10}{15}$

$+ \frac{1}{5} = \frac{3}{15}$

and add.

STOP

1 $17 + 2 =$
A 34
B 15
C 12
D 19
E NH

5 $\$26.07$ $+ \$39.81$
A $65.88
B $66.07
C $68.03
D $76.77
E NH

2 $4.35 \times 76.2 =$
F 331.470
G 80.55
H 303.70
J 3314.70
K NH

6 $62 \div 5 =$

_____

_____

_____

3 $6\frac{3}{8}$ $+ 9\frac{5}{8}$
A 17
B 15
C 16
D $15\frac{7}{8}$
E NH

7 $650 \div 7 =$
F 88 R1
G 90 R2
H 92 R6
J 92 R3
K NH

4 $14 \times 23 =$
F 70
G 308
H 322
J 312
K NH

8 $\frac{7}{8}$ $- \frac{2}{8}$
A $\frac{1}{8}$
B $\frac{1}{2}$
C $\frac{3}{8}$
D $\frac{5}{8}$
E NH

STOP

Answers
SA (A) (B) (C) (D) (E)   2 (F) (G) (H) (J) (K)   4 (F) (G) (H) (J) (K)   7 (F) (G) (H) (J) (K)
1 (A) (B) (C) (D) (E)   3 (A) (B) (C) (D) (E)   5 (A) (B) (C) (D) (E)   8 (A) (B) (C) (D) (E)

73

Directions: Darken the circle for the correct answer. Darken the circle for NH (Not Here) if the correct answer is not given. If no choices are given, write in the answer.

> **TRY THIS**
>
> Read the word problem carefully. Then set up the word problem as a numerical formula. Solve the formula and compare it to the answer choices.

Sample A

Sally mowed 2 lawns today and 3 lawns yesterday. She was paid $3 for each lawn.

How much money did she earn altogether?

A $5

B $10

C $12

D $15

E NH

> **THINK IT THROUGH**
>
> The correct answer is <u>D</u>. Add 2 lawns today and 3 lawns yesterday. This equals 5. Next, multiply $3 × 5. This gives the total of <u>$15</u> earned.

 STOP

---

1 A family of 8 wants to paddle in the canoes at the park. Each boat holds 2 people.

If they all want to ride at the same time, how many canoes will they need?

A 2

B 4

C 6

D 16

E NH

2 Mr. Klein drove his truck 17,234 miles.

What is that number rounded to the nearest thousand miles?

F 16,000

G 16,500

H 17,000

J 18,000

K NH

3 Suki took a trip. She drove 12 miles to the airport and flew 948 miles to Florida. How many miles did she travel in all?

A 747 miles

B 929 miles

C 960 miles

D 1,060 miles

E NH

4 Chairs for the office desks cost $8 each.

Find the total cost of 257 chairs.

_____

_____

_____

STOP

Answers
SA Ⓐ Ⓑ Ⓒ Ⓓ Ⓔ   **1** Ⓐ Ⓑ Ⓒ Ⓓ Ⓔ   **2** Ⓕ Ⓖ Ⓗ Ⓙ Ⓚ   **3** Ⓐ Ⓑ Ⓒ Ⓓ Ⓔ

Sample A

$4\overline{)79}$

A   19

B   19 R3

C   12 R1

D   17 R1

E   NH

STOP

Sample B

Mr. Lyons used $2\frac{1}{2}$ cups of flour for one recipe and $4\frac{2}{3}$ cups of flour for another recipe. How much flour did he use altogether?

F $6\frac{2}{3}$ cups

G $6\frac{5}{8}$ cups

H $7\frac{1}{3}$ cups

J $7\frac{1}{2}$ cups

K   NH

STOP

For questions 1–16, darken the circle for the correct answer. Darken the circle for NH (Not Here) if the correct answer is not given. If no choices are given, write in the answer.

1

$\begin{array}{r} 5.872 \\ -\,0.6821 \\ \hline \end{array}$

A   5.191

B   5.211

C   4.190

D   1.552

E   NH

2

$\frac{7}{11} \times \frac{1}{2}$

F $\frac{8}{13}$

G $\frac{7}{22}$

H $\frac{11}{14}$

J $\frac{3}{22}$

K   NH

3

$\begin{array}{r} \frac{1}{8} \\ +\,\frac{1}{4} \\ \hline \end{array}$

A $\frac{1}{12}$

B $\frac{3}{8}$

C $\frac{1}{4}$

D $\frac{1}{6}$

E   NH

4

$\begin{array}{r} \frac{8}{21} \\ +\,\frac{9}{21} \\ \hline \end{array}$

F $\frac{18}{21}$

G $\frac{17}{24}$

H $\frac{72}{21}$

J $\frac{1}{21}$

K   NH

5

$96 - 79 =$

A   7

B   16

C   17

D   165

E   NH

6

$\frac{7}{8} - \frac{1}{8} =$

F $\frac{5}{8}$

G $\frac{3}{4}$

H $\frac{8}{16}$

J $\frac{2}{4}$

K   NH

7

$600 \div 40 =$

A   150

B   15

C   12

D   640

E   NH

8

$0.5 \times 8 =$

F   40

G   4

H   0.04

J   0.004

K   NH

9 $85 \times 70 =$

_____

_____

_____

GO ON

10 Andy and Nate collect sports-team pennants. Andy has 18 and Nate has 13.

How many more pennants does Andy have than Nate?

A 5

B 21

C 15

D 31

E NH

11 Kenny wants to buy 4 hot dogs and 2 orders of french fries.

How much change will he get from a $20 bill?

hamburger $2

french fries $1

hot dog $1.50

Soda s- $1.00
      L- $1.50

F $11

G $9

H $10

J $8

K NH

12 Sandra bought a package of 320 stickers for each of 15 friends she invited to her party. How many stickers did she buy?

A 4,800

B 3,812

C 1,920

D 4,700

E NH

13 Elizabeth plans to wrap 20 gifts. She needs 2 feet of ribbon for each gift.

How many feet of ribbon does she need?

F 10 feet

G 18 feet

H 40 feet

J 22 feet

K NH

14 Janet plants 20 varieties of flowers in the spring. She reports that 90% of the varieties of flowers she planted have bloomed.

How many varieties have bloomed?

A 19

B 18

C 17

D 9

E NH

15 The Fun Fair sold 1,839 food tickets.

What is this number rounded to the nearest thousand?

F 1,800

G 2,000

H 1,900

J 1,000

K NH

TEST TIP

Try circling key words in questions. In question 15, circle *thousand* to help you remember to round to the correct place.

Answers

10 Ⓐ Ⓑ Ⓒ Ⓓ Ⓔ   12 Ⓐ Ⓑ Ⓒ Ⓓ Ⓔ   14 Ⓐ Ⓑ Ⓒ Ⓓ Ⓔ
11 Ⓕ Ⓖ Ⓗ Ⓙ Ⓚ   13 Ⓕ Ⓖ Ⓗ Ⓙ Ⓚ   15 Ⓕ Ⓖ Ⓗ Ⓙ Ⓚ

STOP

Sample A

Which number sentence is in the same fact family as 3 × 8 = 24?

A 24 − 8 = 16

B 8 + 3 = 11

C 6 × 4 = 24

D 24 ÷ 8 = 3

STOP

For questions 1–50, darken the circle for the correct answer, or write in the answer.

1 Which decimal belongs in the box on the number line?

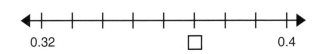

0.32 ☐ 0.4

A 0.37

B 0.38

C 0.36

D 0.35

2 What number makes this number sentence true?

3 × (1 × 9) = (3 × ☐) × 9

F 27

G 13

H 9

J 1

3 What is another way to write 2,078?

A 20 + 70 + 80

B 20 + 78

C 2,000 + 70 + 8

D 2,000 + 7 + 80

4 Last year 567,290 people attended sporting events at the university. How is 567,290 written in words?

F Fifty-six hundred thousand seven twenty-nine

G Fifty-six thousand seven hundred twenty-nine

H Five million sixty-seven thousand two hundred ninety

J Five hundred sixty-seven thousand two hundred ninety

5 In the number 52,658, the 2 means—

A 200

B 20,000

C 2,000

D 20

6 $\frac{14}{18}$ means the same as—

F $\frac{3}{7}$ H $\frac{6}{8}$

G $\frac{5}{9}$ J $\frac{7}{9}$

7 The science class measured 2.56 inches of rain in September, 2.67 inches of rain in October, 2.43 inches of rain in November, and 2.13 inches of rain in December. During which month did it rain most?

A September

B October

C November

D December

8 What is the value of the 3 in 25.430?

_____

_____

_____

_____

GO ON

Answers

SA Ⓐ Ⓑ Ⓒ Ⓓ   **2** Ⓕ Ⓖ Ⓗ Ⓙ   **4** Ⓕ Ⓖ Ⓗ Ⓙ   **6** Ⓕ Ⓖ Ⓗ Ⓙ

1 Ⓐ Ⓑ Ⓒ Ⓓ   **3** Ⓐ Ⓑ Ⓒ Ⓓ   **5** Ⓐ Ⓑ Ⓒ Ⓓ   **7** Ⓐ Ⓑ Ⓒ Ⓓ

9 Mario works in a bakery. He made 90 more loaves of bread on Saturday than he did on Sunday. He made 70 more loaves of bread on Monday than he did on Sunday. If he made 340 loaves of bread on Monday, how many loaves of bread did he make on Saturday?

F 160

G 320

H 360

J 380

10 The school store sells paper with or without binder holes. It is available in white or in yellow. The paper comes in 3 sizes. How many choices of paper do students have when buying paper at the school store?

A 12 choices

B 7 choices

C 6 choices

D 3 choices

11 In which numeral does the 6 stand for 6 tens?

F 3,692

G 6,210

H 364

J 346

12 Carl has 36 fish in the first aquarium and 52 fish in the second aquarium. How many fish should he move to the first aquarium so that both aquariums have an equal number of fish?

A 24

B 16

C 12

D 8

13 Gerald bought 3 shirts for $8.40 each, 2 shirts for $12.89 each, and 1 shirt for $18.90. What was the average cost of the shirts?

F $13.40　　　　H $10.45

G $11.65　　　　J $10.24

14 Which equation could be used to find the number of seconds in a day?

A $60t = 60 + 60$

B $\frac{t}{24} = 60 \times 60$

C $t = (60 \times 60) \div 24$

D $24t = 60 + 60 + 60$

15 If $x = 6$, then $x + 9 =$

F 1　　　　　　H 15

G 10　　　　　J 18

16 Heidi has a choice of 4 colors of paint, 3 kinds of curtains, and 2 colors of carpet to decorate her apartment. How many different combinations of paint, curtains, and carpets can she use?

_____

_____

_____

_____

17 Which problem could be solved by the equation $x = 0.3 \times 200$

A Three hamburgers cost $2.00. How much does one cost?

B The theater holds 200 people. How many people would be able to attend 3 showings of a movie?

C The regular fare of $200 for a plane ticket was just reduced by 30%. What would the savings be?

D The temperature in an oven was 200 degrees. It was then increased by 0.3 degrees. What is the current oven temperature?

GO ON ▶

Answers

9 F G H J　　11 F G H J　　13 F G H J　　15 F G H J

10 A B C D　　12 A B C D　　14 A B C D　　17 A B C D

This graph shows the number of students who eat certain kinds of snacks. Study the graph. Then answer questions 18–20.

STUDENTS' FAVORITE SNACKS

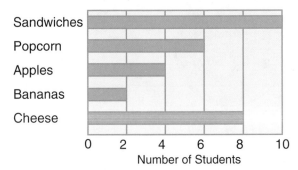

18 What two snacks together are eaten by the same number of students as the number of students who eat popcorn?

F apples and bananas

G bananas and cheese

H apples and sandwiches

J apples and cheese

19 Which of these questions cannot be answered using the information on the graph?

A How many students eat bananas?

B How many more students eat sandwiches than cheese?

C How many students eat two snacks?

D How many fewer students eat popcorn than cheese?

20 If 5 students switched from sandwiches to popcorn, how many students would then eat popcorn?

F 7

G 9

H 11

J 12

The graph below shows the number of students in each grade who ride the bus or walk to school. Study the graph. Then answer questions 21–23.

Methods of Transportation

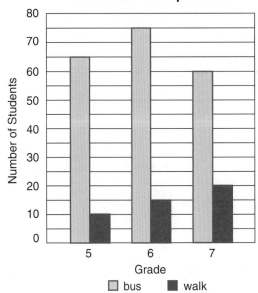

21 How many sixth-grade students ride the bus to school?

A 75   C 60

B 65   D 15

22 If half of the seventh-grade students who take the bus to school start walking to school, how many students would walk to school altogether?

F 55   H 75

G 60   J 80

23 How many students walk to school altogether?

_____

_____

_____

_____

GO ON

Burnet School had a wrapping paper sale. The following graph shows how many rolls of wrapping paper were sold by each grade. Study the graph. Then answer questions 24–26.

WRAPPING PAPER SALES

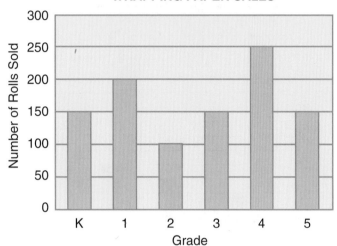

24 How many more rolls of wrapping paper did the fourth grade sell than kindergarten?

　A 100

　B 50

　C 150

　D 200

25 How many rolls of wrapping paper did the first grade sell?

　F 450

　G 200

　H 100

　J 250

26 Which grade sold the fewest rolls of wrapping paper?

　A K

　B 4

　C 2

　D 3

27 Kim's favorite word game uses the spinner shown here. What is the probability that the spinner will land on a vowel?

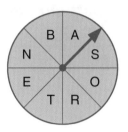

　F $\frac{2}{8}$

　G $\frac{3}{8}$

　H $\frac{4}{8}$

　J $\frac{5}{8}$

28 On four different days, Mrs. Scanlon's fifth-grade class collected 18, 26, 15, and 25 pounds of aluminum cans for recycling. What was the average number of pounds collected during the four days?

_____

_____

_____

_____

29 With his eyes closed, which card will Julio most likely pick?

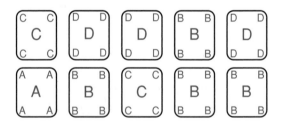

　A A

　B B

　C C

　D D

GO ON

Answers
24 Ⓐ Ⓑ Ⓒ Ⓓ　　**25** Ⓕ Ⓖ Ⓗ Ⓙ　　**26** Ⓐ Ⓑ Ⓒ Ⓓ　　**27** Ⓕ Ⓖ Ⓗ Ⓙ　　**29** Ⓐ Ⓑ Ⓒ Ⓓ

30 A box of 10 computer diskettes costs $23. A reasonable price for a case of 136 of these boxes is —

F less than $1,800.

G between $2,000 and $2,500.

H between $2,500 and $3,500.

J between $3,500 and $4,500.

31 Each month Marty puts $17.00 in his savings account. What is the best estimate of Marty's total savings for 1 year?

A $100.00   C $200.00

B $150.00   D $300.00

32 The figure below shows the picture frame that Felix is making in art class. What is the perimeter of the picture frame?

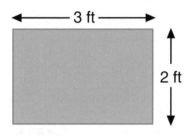

F 6 ft   H 12 ft

G 10 ft   J 20 ft

33 If the pattern formed by the dots continues, how many dots are needed to make the next shape?

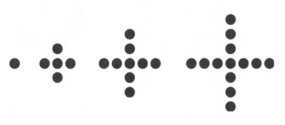

A 14   C 17

B 15   D 20

34 The table shown here represents the relationship between x and y. Based on the relationship shown here, what number belongs in the empty box in row x?

x	7	8	9	10	11	
y	21	24	27	30	33	48

F 12

G 16

H 24

J 30

35 Aunt Lila's rose garden is in the shape of a square. How many feet of edging does she need to go around the entire garden?

12 ft

_____

_____

_____

36 Juan can throw a football 42 yards. He can throw a baseball 109 yards. *About* how much farther can he throw a baseball than a football?

A 60 yards

B 80 yards

C 100 yards

D 150 yards

TEST TIP

The word *about* is a clue that tells you to estimate to find an answer.

GO ON ➡

37 Choose the clock that shows the time 4 hours after 11:00 a.m.

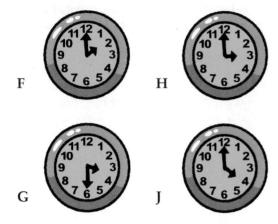

F H

G J

38 What is the area of the rectangle shown?

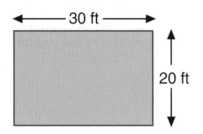

A 50 square feet

B 100 square feet

C 6,000 square feet

D 600 square feet

39 The area of figure A is 1 square unit. What is the area of figure B?

F 4 square units

G 6 square units

H 9 square units

J 12 square units

40 Marsha's soccer team starts its practice at 4:30. It ends at 5:15. How long does Marsha's soccer team practice?

A 15 minutes

B 30 minutes

C 40 minutes

D 45 minutes

41 How many right angles does this figure have?

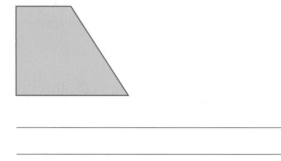

_____

_____

_____

_____

42 The hands of which clock form a right angle?

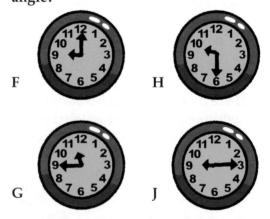

F H

G J

43 Mr. Lan has a greenhouse that is shaped like a rectangle. The length of one short side is 6 meters. The length of one long side is 12 meters. What is the perimeter of his greenhouse?

A 36 meters C 24 meters

B 18 meters D 12 meters

GO ON ➡

Answers

37 Ⓕ Ⓖ Ⓗ Ⓙ   39 Ⓕ Ⓖ Ⓗ Ⓙ   42 Ⓕ Ⓖ Ⓗ Ⓙ

38 Ⓐ Ⓑ Ⓒ Ⓓ   40 Ⓐ Ⓑ Ⓒ Ⓓ   43 Ⓐ Ⓑ Ⓒ Ⓓ

44 Yolanda's herb garden is shaped like a rectangle. How many feet of fencing does she need to go around the entire garden?

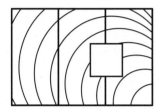

8 ft.

22 ft.

F 16 ft.   H 60 ft.

G 30 ft.   J 176 ft.

45 Which shows the piece missing from the figure?

A   C

B   D

46 Tony's birthday is 20 days before Ann's. Ann's birthday is 7 days after Vic's. Vic's birthday is on the 20th. When is Tony's birthday?

_____

_____

47 Casey bought 3 small spools of string and 1 large spool that had 250 feet of string. What other information is needed to determine how much more string is on the large spool than on the 3 small ones combined?

F the number of inches in a foot

G the kind of string on each spool

H the number of feet of string on 3 large spools

J the number of feet of string on each small spool

48 The students in Longfellow School have decided to take part in their town's food drive. Their goal is to collect 600 cans of food. Each student plans to collect 5 cans. What do you need to know to find out whether the students will be able to reach their goal?

A how many people will provide food

B how many students there are at Longfellow School

C how many grocery stores there are

D how much each can costs

49 Bernie has a sheet of plastic that is 12 feet wide. Alex's sheet of plastic is also 12 feet wide, but it has an area that is 3 times as large as Bernie's. What additional information is needed to find the length of Alex's sheet of plastic?

F the thickness of Bernie's sheet

G the thickness of Alex's sheet

H the combined widths of the two sheets

J the length of Bernie's sheet

50 Marlene has 5 cats. Snowball is smaller than Sugar. Muffin is smaller than Pixy. Shadow is the smallest. Sugar is smaller than Muffin. Which of these is the most reasonable answer?

A Shadow is larger than Sugar.

B Pixy is the largest cat.

C Muffin is smaller than Snowball.

D Snowball is larger than Pixy.

TEST TIP

Try drawing a picture to answer question 50. Draw 5 cats and add their names.

STOP

Answers

44 Ⓕ Ⓖ Ⓗ Ⓙ   **47** Ⓕ Ⓖ Ⓗ Ⓙ   **49** Ⓕ Ⓖ Ⓗ Ⓙ

45 Ⓐ Ⓑ Ⓒ Ⓓ   **48** Ⓐ Ⓑ Ⓒ Ⓓ   **50** Ⓐ Ⓑ Ⓒ Ⓓ

LANGUAGE

═══ PREWRITING, COMPOSING, AND EDITING ═══

Directions: Read each sentence carefully. Then darken the circle for the correct answer to each question, or write in the answer.

TRY THIS	Pretend that you are writing each sentence. Use the rules you have learned for capitalization, punctuation, word usage, and sentence structure to choose the correct answer.

Sample A

Going Camping

Jeremy knows that many of his classmates are interested in camping. He has been camping many times and knows a lot about it. He wants to write an article for the school newspaper that will give students some camping tips.

Jeremy wants to find out if there is a camping supply store in his neighborhood. He should look in—

A an encyclopedia.

B a telephone directory.

C an atlas.

D a dictionary

THINK IT THROUGH	The correct answer is <u>B</u>. The telephone directory would have the address and telephone number of camping supply stores.

The Hopi Indians

While Alexis was on vacation in Arizona, she learned about Native Americans who live there. She visited a museum that showed how the Hopi Indians lived. She wants to tell her grandmother about what she learned. She decides to write her a letter.

Dear Grandma,

    Hopi Indians lived in the southwest part
    (1)
of the United States. This part is now
        (2)
Arizona. Hopi Indians were always growing
     (3)
their own crops for food.

1   **What is the best way to write sentence 3?**

A   Hopi Indians were planning to grow their own crops for food.

B   Hopi Indians grew their own crops for food.

C   Hopi Indians will be eating their own crops for food.

D   As it is written.

GO ON ➡

Answers
SA Ⓐ Ⓑ Ⓒ Ⓓ   **1** Ⓐ Ⓑ Ⓒ Ⓓ

Study the Table of Contents and Index from a book Jeremy found about camping. Then answer questions 2–6.

Table of Contents

Index

2 Which chapter should Jeremy read to find ideas for making tasty breakfasts when camping?

_____

_____

_____

_____

3 Which pages would have information about types of campgrounds available in national parks?

F 8–15

G 16–18

H 19–22

J 29–30

4 Which chapter should Jeremy read to help him explain about the kinds of sleeping bags used for camping?

A Chapter 1

B Chapter 2

C Chapter 3

D Chapter 4

5 Which page most likely would have information about how to deal with injuries on a camping trip?

F 36

G 37

H 53

J 70

6 Chapter 5 has information on all of the following except—

A where to place the tent.

B where to place the sleeping bags.

C what to place in the cooking area.

D what to do for poison ivy.

GO ON ▶

Answers

3 Ⓕ Ⓖ Ⓗ Ⓙ   4 Ⓐ Ⓑ Ⓒ Ⓓ   5 Ⓕ Ⓖ Ⓗ Ⓙ   6 Ⓐ Ⓑ Ⓒ Ⓓ

Here is a rough draft of the first part of Jeremy's article. Read the rough draft carefully. Then answer questions 7–14.

Going Camping

Have you ever been camping? I can tell you that camping can be fun
(1)   (2)

and exciting. It can be enjoyable. It gives you a chance to experience the
(3)   (4)

outdoors. For example, an example of this are smells, sights, and sounds
(5)

in the outdoors that you can never find in a town or a city. Yellowstone
(6)

National Park has some great campsites. You can enjoy swimming,
(7)

canoeing, and hiking. You can spend time and have fun with your family
(8)

and friends. And your pets.
(9)

Camping is also an affordable way to go on vacation. A campsite costs
(10)   (11)

about $15 and just as eating at home you can have meals for about the

same cost. You can cook these meals on an open fire or cook them on a
(12)

camp stove.

---

7 Which group of words is not a complete sentence?

F 3

G 9

H 11

J 12

8 What is the topic sentence of the second paragraph?

A 12

B 11

C 10

D 1

GO ON

9 Which of the following sentences best combines sentence 2 and sentence 3 without changing their meaning?

    F I can tell you a lot about camping, fun, exciting, enjoyable.

    G I can tell you that camping can be things such as fun, exciting, and enjoyable.

    H I can tell you that camping can be fun, exciting, and enjoyable.

    J Fun, exciting, and enjoyable is what I can tell you that camping is.

10 What is the best way to write sentence 5?

    A An example of an example are smells, sights, and sounds that you can never find in a town or a city.

    B There are smells, sights, and sounds in the outdoors that you can never find in a town or a city.

    C There are smell, sights, and sounds in the outdoors, for example, that are different than the smell, sights, and sounds in a city.

    D As it is written.

11 Which of the following sentences could be added before sentence 7?

    F My favorite part of camping is roasting marshmallows.

    G There are many activities you can enjoy.

    H While camping, everyone dresses comfortably.

    J My family usually goes camping four or five times a year.

12 The best way to write sentence 11 is—

    A A campsite costs $15 and for about as much as you eat at home will cost you camping.

    B A campsite is about $15 and meals are about the same as at home.

    C A campsite costs about $15, and meals cost about the same as eating at home.

    D As it is written.

13 What is the most colorful way to write sentence 12?

    F You can cook delicious meals on a crackling open fire or cook them on a camp stove.

    G You can cook meals on a fire or a stove.

    H You can cook some of the meals on a fire and some on a stove.

    J As it is written.

14 Which sentence contains information that does not belong in Jeremy's article? Write the number of the sentence.

_____

_____

_____

GO ON

Answers

    9 Ⓕ Ⓖ Ⓗ Ⓙ   **10** Ⓐ Ⓑ Ⓒ Ⓓ   **11** Ⓕ Ⓖ Ⓗ Ⓙ   **12** Ⓐ Ⓑ Ⓒ Ⓓ   **13** Ⓕ Ⓖ Ⓗ Ⓙ

Here is the next part of Jeremy's rough draft for his article. This part has certain words and phrases underlined. Read the draft carefully. Then answer questions 15–22.

To have the <u>best time camping plan ahead.</u> Choose a campground
            (13)   **(14)**

carefully. <u>You needs to know</u> what you plan to do there and how to get
              (15)

there. There are many different campgrounds available. Some
   (16)   **(17)**

campgrounds may have a first-come, first-served policy, but at other

campgrounds you may have to make reservations.

<u>Once you chose</u> a campground, you need to have the right equipment.
   (18)

The most important <u>equipment are the tent.</u> A tent keeps you dry, gave
   (19)   **(20)**

<u>you shelter and protects</u> you from insects. The tent should be one that
                  (21)

you and your family can handle easily. <u>There is many kinds</u> of tents to
                                      (22)

choose from. It <u>might be a good idea</u> to rent a tent for your first camping
               (23)

trip. This <u>gave</u> you a chance to see how you like camping.
       (24)

15 In sentence 13, <u>best time camping plan</u> is best written—

A best time camping, plan

B best, time camping plan

C best time, camping plan

D As it is written.

16 In sentence 15, <u>You needs to know</u> is best written—

F Yous need to know

G You need to know

H You needed to know

J As it is written.

GO ON

Answers
15 Ⓐ Ⓑ Ⓒ Ⓓ   **16** Ⓕ Ⓖ Ⓗ Ⓙ

17 In sentence 18, <u>Once you chose</u> is best written—

    A Once you chooses

    B Once you chosen

    C Once you choose

    D As it is written.

18 In sentence 19, <u>equipment are the tent</u> is best written—

    F equipments are the tent

    G equipment is the tent

    H equipments is the tent

    J As it is written.

19 In sentence 20, <u>gave you shelter and protects</u> is best written—

    A gives you shelter, and protects

    B gives you shelter and, protects

    C gives you shelters and protects

    D As it is written.

20 In sentence 22, <u>There is many kinds</u> is best written—

    F There were many kinds

    G There is many kind

    H There are many kinds

    J As it is written.

21 In sentence 23, <u>might be a good idea</u> is best written—

    A was a good idea

    B might have been a good idea

    C might been a good idea

    D As it is written.

22 In sentence 24, <u>gave</u> is best written—

    F given

    G will give

    H gaves

    J As it is written.

STOP

Answers

17 Ⓐ Ⓑ Ⓒ Ⓓ   **19** Ⓐ Ⓑ Ⓒ Ⓓ   **21** Ⓐ Ⓑ Ⓒ Ⓓ

18 Ⓕ Ⓖ Ⓗ Ⓙ   **20** Ⓕ Ⓖ Ⓗ Ⓙ   **22** Ⓕ Ⓖ Ⓗ Ⓙ

Directions: Read each sentence carefully. If one of the words is misspelled, darken the circle for that word. If all the words are spelled correctly, then darken the circle for *No mistake*.

TRY THIS Read each sentence carefully. If you are not sure of an answer, first decide which answer choices are spelled correctly. Then see if you can recognize the misspelled word from your reading experience.

Sample A

The <u>pair</u> Mother gave me was <u>ripe</u> and <u>juicy</u>. <u>No mistake</u>
   A   B   C   D

THINK IT THROUGH The correct answer is <u>A</u>. A piece of fruit is spelled <u>pear</u>.

STOP

1. Ms. Coe <u>clutched</u> her <u>purse</u> <u>tightly</u>. <u>No mistake</u>
              A   B   C   D

2. Jody took a long <u>trek</u> <u>through</u> the <u>meadows</u>. <u>No mistake</u>
                     F   G   H   J

3. The boys <u>observed</u> the <u>striped</u> <u>caterpiller</u> move along the leaf. <u>No mistake</u>
              A   B   C   D

4. The <u>satelite</u> was <u>orbiting</u> the <u>earth</u>. <u>No mistake</u>
         F   G   H   J

5. The iron <u>filings</u> were <u>atracted</u> to the <u>magnet</u>. <u>No mistake</u>
            A   B   C   D

6. John <u>disliked</u> doing his <u>algebra</u> <u>homework</u>. <u>No mistake</u>
        F   G   H   J

7. Taki was <u>familier</u> with the <u>rules</u> of the <u>game</u>. <u>No mistake</u>
              A   B   C   D

8. Percy was <u>breathles</u> from <u>running</u> the <u>race</u>. <u>No mistake</u>
           F   G   H   J

STOP

Answers
SA Ⓐ Ⓑ Ⓒ Ⓓ   2 Ⓕ Ⓖ Ⓗ Ⓙ   4 Ⓕ Ⓖ Ⓗ Ⓙ   6 Ⓕ Ⓖ Ⓗ Ⓙ   8 Ⓕ Ⓖ Ⓗ Ⓙ
1 Ⓐ Ⓑ Ⓒ Ⓓ   3 Ⓐ Ⓑ Ⓒ Ⓓ   5 Ⓐ Ⓑ Ⓒ Ⓓ   7 Ⓐ Ⓑ Ⓒ Ⓓ

Save the Earth

Santina's school is celebrating Earth Day. She knows it is important to conserve resources. She wants to do a report about recycling. She hopes that the report will encourage everyone to recycle.

Santina wants to include a definition of the word <u>recycling</u>. Which guide words might mark the page on which she would find it?

A recognize–recount

B recess–recognize

C recourse–red

D rebound–reception

Here is a rough draft of the first part of Santina's report. Read the rough draft carefully. Then answer questions 1–7.

Save the Earth

I think that Earth Day is a good time to think about our planet, our
(1)

planet Earth. People who lived long ago enjoyed clean air, clean water,
(2)

and open land. In the past couple of hundred years. These things have
(3)   (4)

changed. Our country was just starting two hundred years ago.
(5)

Today, the air and water are polluted the land is filled with things
(6)

that people throw away. Some of our garbage is loaded with dangerous
(7)

chemicals. These chemicals are dangerous for both people and animals.
(8)

To decrease this kind of pollution, we have to learn to care about our
(9)

environment. We either have to find ways to properly dispose of dangerous
(10)

chemicals or stop making the products that produce the chemicals.

Answers
SA Ⓐ Ⓑ Ⓒ Ⓓ

1 Which words are <u>not</u> a complete thought?

    A 3

    B 4

    C 5

    D 6

2 What is the best way to write sentence 1?

    F I think that Earth Day is a good time to think about Earth our planet.

    G I think that Earth Day is a good time to think about our planet.

    H I think that Earth Day is a good day to think about our Earth planet.

    J As it is written.

3 What is the most colorful way to write sentence 2?

    A People who lived long ago enjoyed clean air, water, and land.

    B People who lived long ago enjoyed clean-smelling air, pure water, and uncluttered land.

    C People enjoyed air, water, and land that was clean.

    D As it is written.

4 Which sentence needs to be made into more than one sentence? Write the number of the sentence.

_____

_____

_____

_____

5 Which sentence does <u>not</u> belong in Santina's report?

    F 2

    G 3

    H 4

    J 5

6 Which of the following sentences best combines sentence 3 and sentence 4 without changing their meaning?

    A These things have been changed, in the past couple of hundred years.

    B In the past couple of hundred years, these things have changed.

    C In the couple of hundred years past these things have changed.

    D Things have changed these, in the past couple of hundred years.

7 What supporting information could be added after sentence 6?

    F Many trees have to be cut down to make paper for newspapers.

    G People in other countries also have problems with pollution.

    H The word *environment* means "the world around us."

    J More landfills are being built to hold this garbage.

GO ON

Answers

1 Ⓐ Ⓑ Ⓒ Ⓓ   **3** Ⓐ Ⓑ Ⓒ Ⓓ   **6** Ⓐ Ⓑ Ⓒ Ⓓ

2 Ⓕ Ⓖ Ⓗ Ⓙ   **5** Ⓕ Ⓖ Ⓗ Ⓙ   **7** Ⓕ Ⓖ Ⓗ Ⓙ

Here is the next part of Santina's rough draft for her report. This part has certain words and phrases underlined. Read the draft carefully. Then answer questions 8–16.

I think recycling is a great way to decrease garbage and save natural
(11)

resources. When items are recycled, they can be used again or made into
(12)

something new. Many items can be recycled. For example, <u>aunt Jane's</u>
(13)   (14)

aluminum <u>cans the ones she saves</u>, can be recycled. <u>Plastic bottles</u>
(15)

<u>newspapers and jars</u> are other things that can be recycled. By recycling
(16)

these things, we stop them from ending up as garbage.

How can we participate in recycling? There are a couple of ways. <u>Our</u>
(17)   (18)   (19)

<u>towns recycling program</u> makes recycling easy. Every house <u>have</u> a green
(20)

box for collecting recyclable goods. Every week a <u>recycling truck picked</u>
(21)

<u>up</u> the materials <u>that residents leave by the curb</u> in the box. Other towns
(22)

have recycling centers. People <u>can drop off recyclable goods</u> at these
(23)

centers. Recycling <u>is a sensible, easy solution</u> to caring for our planet.
(24)

8 In sentence 14, <u>cans the ones she saves</u> is best written—

   A cans the ones, she saves,

   B cans the, ones she saves,

   C cans, the ones she saves,

   D As it is written.

9 In sentence 14, <u>aunt Jane's</u> is best written—

   F aunt janes

   G Aunt Janes

   H Aunt Jane's

   J As it is written

GO ON

Answers
8 Ⓐ Ⓑ Ⓒ Ⓓ   9 Ⓕ Ⓖ Ⓗ Ⓙ

10 In sentence 15, <u>Plastic bottles newspapers and jars</u> is best written—

A Plastic bottles, newspapers, and jars

B Plastic, bottles, newspapers and, jars

C Plastic, bottles, newspapers, and jars

D As it is written.

11 In sentence 19, <u>Our towns recycling program</u> is best written—

F Our towns' recycling program

G Our town's recycling program

H Our towns's recycling program

J As it is written.

12 In sentence 20, <u>Every house have</u> is best written—

A Every house having

B Every houses have

C Every house has

D As it is written.

13 In sentence 21, <u>that residents leave by the curb</u> is best written—

F that residents are leaving by the curb

G that residents left by the curb

H that, by the curb, residents leave

J As it is written.

14 In sentence 21, <u>recycling truck picked up</u> is best written—

A recycling truck picks up

B recycling truck picking up

C recycling truck had picked up

D As it is written.

15 In sentence 23, <u>can drop off recyclable goods</u> is best written—

F will drop off recyclable goods

G dropping off recyclable goods

H dropped off recyclable goods

J As it is written.

16 In sentence 24, <u>is a sensible, easy solution</u> is best written—

A is a sensible, easier solution

B is a sensible and easier solution

C is a sensible solution and easy

D As it is written.

GO ON

For questions 17–28, read each sentence carefully. If one of the words is misspelled, darken the circle for that word. If all of the words are spelled correctly, then darken the circle for *No mistake*.

17   Marcus thought that Tim's piano resital was boring. No mistake
                             F   G   H   J

18   They were marooned on a dessert island. No mistake
                     A   B   C   D

19   My little sister Caroline was borne on Christmas. No mistake
           F   G   H   J

20   The sponge absorbed the liquid that she spilled. No mistake
             A   B   C   D

21   The adjective modifys the noun in that sentence. No mistake
             F   G   H   J

22   Veronica sprented to the finish line and won the race. No mistake
                   A   B   C   D

23   The conplete edition has ten volumes. No mistake
             F   G   H   J

24   Springfield is the capitol of Illinois. No mistake
             A   B   C   D

25   Jamal lived abroad when he was younger. No mistake
             F   G   H   J

26   Noriko spoke to the commisioner at the banquet. No mistake
                   A   B   C   D

27   The vault door closed automatecally behind the bank guard. No mistake
             F   G   H   J

28   The otter sliped down the riverbank and splashed into the water. No mistake
             A   B   C   D

STOP

Answers
17 Ⓕ Ⓖ Ⓗ Ⓙ   20 Ⓐ Ⓑ Ⓒ Ⓓ   23 Ⓕ Ⓖ Ⓗ Ⓙ   26 Ⓐ Ⓑ Ⓒ Ⓓ
18 Ⓐ Ⓑ Ⓒ Ⓓ   21 Ⓕ Ⓖ Ⓗ Ⓙ   24 Ⓐ Ⓑ Ⓒ Ⓓ   27 Ⓕ Ⓖ Ⓗ Ⓙ
19 Ⓕ Ⓖ Ⓗ Ⓙ   22 Ⓐ Ⓑ Ⓒ Ⓓ   25 Ⓕ Ⓖ Ⓗ Ⓙ   28 Ⓐ Ⓑ Ⓒ Ⓓ

READING COMPREHENSION

Use the removable answer sheet on page 127 to record your answers for the practice tests.

Sample A

Polar Bears

Polar bears are sometimes called ice bears or snow bears. These huge bears live in the icy lands near the North Pole. They sometimes weigh more than 1,000 pounds. Their thick, white fur and layers of fat help them stay warm in freezing winters. Polar bears live by themselves except when a mother has cubs.

Why can polar bears live near the North Pole?

A They build fires.

B They huddle close together.

C They stay in caves all winter.

D They have thick fur and layers of fat.

For questions 1–40, carefully read each selection and the questions that follow. Then darken the circle for the correct answer, or write in the answer.

Fishing

David and Fumio take their canoe out after supper to fish for bass. As the sun starts to go down, a symphony rises from the lake. Insects buzz, frogs croak, and birds chirp a chorus. The boys give up fishing and enjoy the *natural wonders* around them. A snapping turtle glides near the boat. It submerges and resurfaces, then submerges again, a natural submarine. Its periscope neck sticks up through the surface of the water. Then with a splash, the turtle's head disappears.

"I think it's time for us to leave, too." David says. Both boys are smiling.

1 **"A symphony rises from the lake" means—**

A some musicians have come to play.

B birds, insects, and frogs make many different noises as night falls.

C lakes are musical places.

D Fumio is playing his portable radio.

2 **Why do David and Fumio go to the lake?**

_____

_____

_____

_____

3 **The snapping turtle was like a submarine because—**

F it had the shape of a submarine.

G it went under the water and had a "periscope" neck.

H it was the color of a submarine.

J submarines make a snapping sound.

4 **What are the <u>natural wonders</u>?**

_____

_____

_____

GO ON

An Interesting Collection

Erica's grandfather, Max, was a sailor. He traveled all over the world. When he traveled, he collected shells. Now he has shells from many different places.

Erica always admired her grandfather's shells. When she was nine years old, she started her own shell collection. She hopes to have a collection like her grandfather's someday. She knows it will take a long time.

Erica collects shells from the shores of rivers, seas, lakes, and streams. Sometimes she finds shells in dry places that used to be underwater. Most of the shells that she collects belong to a group of animals known as mollusks. Snails, clams, and oysters are all mollusks.

Each animal's shell differs in shape as well as in size and color. A snail's shell is one piece. It is like a tube that winds around itself as it grows. Clams and oysters have shells made of two parts joined together at one spot. Clams and oysters can keep their shells open when they are resting. Other mollusks have shells called tooth shells. These shells look like long needles.

Erica has been collecting shells for three years. She has almost one hundred shells. Max told her it was time to learn how to care for her collection properly. He taught Erica how to clean her shells. She boils them in water for five to ten minutes. Then she washes the shells in soap and water. Finally she puts the shells on pieces of cardboard. On each piece of cardboard, she writes down the name of the shell and when and where she found it.

Now Erica and her grandfather go looking for shells together. Erica even has one or two shells that her grandfather doesn't have. There are so many kinds of shells that both of their collections will keep growing for a long time.

GO ON

5 All of the following are facts that Erica records on the pieces of cardboard *except*—

A the kind of shell.

B where the shell was found.

C the date the shell was found.

D the shape of the shell.

6 Erica probably would find shells near all of the following *except*—

F the shore of a lake.

G an ocean beach.

H a swimming pool.

J a stream.

7 This selection is *mainly* about—

A Erica's hobby of collecting shells.

B Erica's grandfather's travels.

C Erica's search for shells.

D the benefits of collecting shells.

8 Which shells can open and close?

_____

_____

_____

_____

_____

9 How old is Erica now?

F nine years old

G ten years old

H twelve years old

J six years old

10 According to the selection, Erica's grandfather taught her—

A where to find shells.

B the names of the animals that live in the shells.

C how to avoid tooth shells.

D how to clean shells.

11 According to the selection, why did Erica want a shell collection?

F She liked her grandfather's collection.

G She liked shells.

H She wanted to travel around the world.

J She liked to eat clams and oysters.

12 Which of the following could be another title for this selection?

A "Erica's Grandfather Max"

B "Erica's Hobby"

C "All About Mollusks"

D "Taking Care of a Shell Collection"

13 According to the selection, how are snail shells and clam shells different?

F Snail shells are found only by lakes.

G Clam shells are produced by mollusks.

H Clam shells cannot be preserved.

J Snail shells are one-piece shells.

14 What is the *next* thing Erica does with her shells after she gathers them?

_____

_____

_____

_____

_____

GO ON ➡

Making a Snow Cave

For those who enjoy cross-country skiing and hiking during the winter months, the following information on building a snow cave may prove *invaluable*.

Directions

1. First, find a deep snowdrift.
2. Next, dig a tunnel into the drift, angling it upward several feet.
3. Then, *excavate* a dome-shaped room at the top of the tunnel, judging the thickness of the roof by watching from the inside for the snow to turn a light blue color. This color tells you that the wall is the correct thickness.
4. Smooth the curved ceiling to remove sharp edges that could cause moisture to drip onto your gear.
5. Next, carve little shelves or spaces in the walls for candles.
6. Then, use a ski pole or a sharp stick to punch holes in the roof at a 45° angle to the floor. Holes made at this angle will allow fresh air in without allowing moisture to enter the dome.
7. Finally, fashion a door by piling snow on a ground cloth, gathering up the four corners, and tying them with a cord. Allow the snow to crystallize into a hard ball that can be pulled with the cloth into the entranceway to block the wind and trap warm air inside the cave.

The cave will probably take two people about two hours to build. Be sure to have a shovel included in your gear, in case a snowdrift blocks the entrance to your snow cave. You can use the shovel to dig an emergency exit.

GO ON

15 If you wanted to learn more about winter camping, you should—

A visit a ski resort.

B look for books on this subject in your library.

C take a winter vacation.

D visit a sporting goods store.

16 The word "excavate" in this selection means to—

F hollow out.

G exclude.

H discover.

J calculate.

17 What does the word "invaluable" mean in this selection?

_____

_____

_____

_____

18 Besides serving as a door to block the cave entryway, the crystallized snow on the cloth—

A can be used as a freezer for food supplies.

B stores drinking water.

C traps warm air in the cave.

D supports the roof of the cave.

19 According to the selection, a shovel can be an important tool to have in a snow cave if you—

F need to dig an emergency exit.

G fight off a wild animal.

H need a support for the ceiling of the snow cave.

J have to dig for food.

20 Shelves are carved into the walls of the snow cave to—

A let in fresh air.

B make windows in the cave.

C support the roof.

D hold candles for lighting the cave.

21 How do you know when the cave walls are the correct thickness?

F Look for a blue color on the walls.

G Test the wall with your shovel.

H Try to punch a hole in the wall.

J This information is not stated in the selection.

22 The directions for making a snow cave help the reader to—

A realize that a snow cave is a permanent shelter.

B see that the author is very well read.

C survive in the winter.

D understand the steps involved in making a snow cave.

GO ON ➡

Tepees: Native American Homes

The Great Plains stretch from Texas to Canada and from the Rocky Mountains to the Missouri River valley. For many years this huge area was nothing but flat grassland. Hawks, elk, deer, coyotes, and bears lived there. Of the many animals on the Great Plains, the most plentiful was the buffalo. One herd might have several million buffaloes.

The Native Americans who lived on the Great Plains followed the buffaloes. They used them for food, clothing, tools, and fuel. For this reason, they needed homes that were light and easy to move. The Sioux, Dakota, Crow, Cheyenne, and Blackfoot peoples all lived in tepees.

No one knows when tepees were first used, but the Spanish explorer Coronado saw them in 1541. Tepees were made from wooden poles tied together in a cone shape. Buffalo hides were sewn together as a covering for the poles. The tepees were warm in winter, dry in rainstorms, and sturdy enough to withstand heavy winds.

Because there were very few trees on the Great Plains, it was difficult to get the long straight poles needed for the tepees. The Cheyenne sometimes traveled from Oklahoma to Montana to get lodge poles. These poles were highly valued. Sometimes a horse would be traded for five poles. The average tepee needed about fifteen poles. The largest tepees used more than thirty.

The women owned the tepees and did most of the work in building them. They took the bark off the poles and let them dry for about three weeks. Meanwhile the cover was made. Twelve to fourteen buffalo hides usually were needed. First, all the fat was scraped off the hides. Then they were left out in the sun to dry for a few days. Next, the hides had to be tanned with a special mixture made from bark, grease, and water. Then they were dried again. Later, the skins were stretched and rubbed to soften them.

Often the woman who owned a tepee held a feast. This was her way of asking the other women to help her. Some women would prepare the buffalo *sinew*, or tissue, that was used as thread. Others cut the hides and then sewed them together.

When it was finished, the new cover was soft, smooth, and white. Then the women hung the cover over the tepee poles and built a fire inside. The smoke would waterproof the cover. The Native Americans usually decorated the tepees with meaningful symbols and designs. Often they recorded the history of an earlier family member on the tepee. The Native Americans used colorful paints made from plants and roots found in their surroundings.

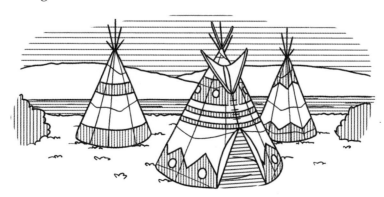

GO ON➡

23 You would most likely find this selection in a—

F   history book.

G   travel magazine.

H   literature textbook.

J   health magazine.

24 What was the *first* step in preparing the buffalo hides as tepee covers?

A   The hides were sewn together.

B   The fat was scraped off the hides.

C   The hides were left in the sun to dry.

D   The hides were tanned with a special mixture.

25 In line 3 of the sixth paragraph, the word "sinew" means—

F   the lodge poles used to build tepees.

G   bark removed from lodge poles.

H   plants and roots used for paint.

J   buffalo tissue used as thread to sew hides together.

26 Which of these statements expresses an *opinion* from the selection?

A   Tepees were the best homes ever invented.

B   Tepees were often decorated with meaningful symbols and designs.

C   Tepees were first used in the 1600s.

D   Tepees were used for many different purposes.

27 There is enough information in the selection to suggest that—

F   tepees were not practical on the Great Plains.

G   Native Americans respected and made good use of their environment.

H   most Native Americans made their living by farming.

J   Native Americans held many colorful celebrations.

28 The Great Plains are located from—

A   the Cascade to the Rocky Mountains.

B   Oregon to California.

C   the Rocky Mountains to the Missouri River valley.

D   Maine to Florida.

29 The web shows some important ideas in the selection.

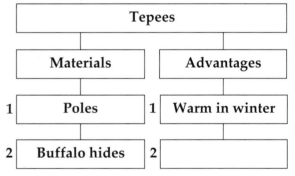

Which belongs in the empty box?

F   Wet in rainstorms

G   Difficult to make

H   Easy to move

J   Owned by women

30 Why was it hard to find poles for tepees?

_____

_____

_____

_____

GO ON ➡

Carnival Fun!

Mercer School is having a Spring Carnival on Saturday and Sunday, April 20 and 21. The carnival will take place on the school playground. It will begin at 11:00 A.M. and end at 5:00 P.M. each day.

Dozens of booths will feature food and handmade items for sale. Everyone will enjoy the entertainment. A children's comedy show will be provided. There will also be live music. All children can enjoy a pony ride. There will be many games, including a three-legged race and a ring toss. All money raised at the carnival will help to fund the Children's Summer Day Camp.

For more information or to buy tickets, call Ms. Díaz, the carnival chairperson, at the school between 8:00 A.M. and 1:00 P.M on school days.

---

31 **If the author added a sentence to the end of the second paragraph, which of these would fit best?**

A   No one will be allowed on the school playground the day before the carnival.

B   For information about selling tickets, call the chairperson.

C   This camp is open to all students at Mercer School.

D   Mercer School teaches students in grades 5 through 8.

32 **There is enough information in this selection to show that—**

F   the carnival is for senior citizens only.

G   the carnival events will especially interest teen-agers.

H   there will be events to interest people of all ages.

J   the carnival is for small children only.

33 **Which of these states an *opinion*?**

A   The carnival will take place on the school playground.

B   Everyone will enjoy the entertainment.

C   The carnival will begin at 11:00 A.M. each day.

D   Dozens of booths will feature food and handmade items for sale.

34 **Where would this selection most likely be found?**

F   in a public library

G   in a national magazine

H   in a school bulletin

J   in a science textbook

35 **When will the carnival take place?**

_____

_____

_____

_____

_____

36 **According to the announcement, the carnival is being held to raise money for—**

A   the children's comedy show.

B   the Children's Summer Day Camp.

C   the Mercer School PTA.

D   winners of the three-legged race.

GO ON➡

A Terrible Flood

The newspaper headlines claimed that the recent flood was a once-in-a-lifetime event. People in the soggy farm town in Iowa certainly hoped that was true. The Mississippi River knew no banks for two weeks in August. The mess that was left behind would take an incredible amount of time, money, and energy to clean.

When Dawn and Greg arrived on the bus at their grandmother's farm town, they didn't recognize much. They saw a lot of rubbish, including parts of homes, pieces of furniture, piles of sandbags, and acres of slimy mud. Here and there they could even see dead fish that had been left behind when the waters *receded*.

Grandmother was anxious to greet Dawn and Greg and get back to the house to start their discouraging clean-up chores. Her car had been ruined in the flood, so they walked the mile to the house.

"Grandma, how badly damaged was your house?" asked Dawn as they slopped through the mud.

"Well, the house is still standing, but it is covered with the same kind of slimy mud we're walking in," replied Grandma.

"You mean this mud came through the doors and windows?" asked Greg incredulously.

"I'm afraid the force of the water and mud broke the basement windows and filled the house up to the second story with river water, silt, and fish," said Grandma sadly.

37 Why did Grandma, Dawn, and Greg walk the mile to Grandma's house?

_____

_____

_____

_____

_____

38 The author included the sixth paragraph to show the reader that—

F Greg wasn't surprised about the damage to Grandma's house.

G Greg couldn't believe what his grandmother told him about the damage to her house.

H Greg wasn't listening to his grandmother.

J Greg couldn't hear what his grandmother was saying.

39 According to the selection, why didn't Dawn and Greg recognize their grandmother's town?

A They had never been there before.

B They hadn't visited there in many years.

C The flood had severely damaged the town.

D The town had been remodeled after the flood.

40 In line 5 of the second paragraph, the word "receded" means—

F advanced.

G rose.

H flooded.

J withdrew.

STOP

READING VOCABULARY

Sample A

Fabric is a kind of—

A cloth   C package

B box   D factory

STOP

For questions 1–8, darken the circle for the word or group of words that has the same or almost the same meaning as the underlined word.

1 To **pursue** is to—

A lead

B stop

C find

D follow

2 **Perpetual** means—

F fades in sunlight

G lasts forever

H foreign

J priceless

3 Something that is **meager** is—

A hearty

B fattening

C skimpy

D silly

4 Something that is **trivial** is—

F important

G large

H unimportant

J confusing

5 Something that is **wrinkled** is—

A dirty

B creased

C pretty

D closed

6 To **combine** means to—

F separate

G blend

H package

J spend

7 Something that is **dismal** is—

A gloomy

B bright

C windy

D happy

8 **Elderly** means—

F old

G young

H new

J friendly

Write your answer to the following:

9 **Absurd** means—

_____

_____

_____

_____

GO ON

Sample B

> The gardeners will <u>deposit</u> the soil in the backyard.

In which sentence does <u>deposit</u> have the same meaning as it does in the sentence above?

A   Zoe put a <u>deposit</u> down on the dress.

B   I will <u>deposit</u> the stack of books on your porch.

C   Rachel wanted to <u>deposit</u> her earnings in her bank.

D   The miners found a <u>deposit</u> of gold.

STOP

For questions 10–14, darken the circle for the sentence in which the underlined word means the same as it does in the sentence in the box.

10

> Jamie had to <u>force</u> his way through the crowd.

In which sentence does <u>force</u> have the same meaning as it does in the sentence above?

A   The <u>force</u> of the explosion blew out the windows in the building.

B   Don't <u>force</u> the child to play.

C   The <u>force</u> of gravity keeps things in place on Earth.

D   We had to <u>force</u> the puppy through the hole in the fence.

11

> We studied the <u>culture</u> of the ancient Egyptians.

In which sentence does <u>culture</u> have the same meaning as it does in the sentence above?

F   Her family's customs are influenced by the Spanish <u>culture</u>.

G   The scientist grew the <u>culture</u> overnight.

H   She is a person with <u>culture</u>, who writes poetry and plays the piano.

J   The doctor took a throat <u>culture</u> from Stella and her brother.

12

> The <u>key</u> to good health is exercise.

In which sentence does <u>key</u> have the same meaning as it does in the sentence above?

A   Make sure you don't lose your <u>key</u>.

B   The choir was singing off <u>key</u>.

C   Max found the <u>key</u> to the mystery.

D   She needed to get the piano <u>key</u> fixed.

13

> To start the machine, <u>press</u> the red button.

In which sentence does <u>press</u> have the same meaning as it does in the sentence above?

F   Can you <u>press</u> this shirt for me?

G   The governor's speech was reported by the <u>press</u>.

H   The chef needed to use a garlic <u>press</u> .

J   <u>Press</u> the elevator button for the third floor.

14

> Grandpa showed us how to <u>pitch</u> horseshoes.

In which sentence does <u>pitch</u> have the same meaning as it does in the sentence above?

A   The campers had to <u>pitch</u> their tents before nightfall.

B   Mandy's instrument was off <u>pitch</u>.

C   Mary's sister learned to <u>pitch</u> at baseball practice.

D   The heavy storm caused the sailboat to <u>pitch</u>.

GO ON

Sample C

She gave a <u>feeble</u> excuse for not completing her homework. <u>Feeble</u> means—

A good

B strong

C believable

D weak

STOP

For questions 15–20, darken the circle for the word or words that give the meaning of the underlined word.

15 The teacher <u>perceived</u> that the confused students did not grasp the lesson. <u>Perceived</u> means—

F understood

G remembered

H begged

J expected

16 Nate soon tired of the <u>tedious</u> work he had been assigned. <u>Tedious</u> means—

A exciting

B computer

C boring

D complicated

17 The little boy cried when the tower he was building <u>collapsed</u>. <u>Collapsed</u> means—

F blew up

G sold out

H fell down

J went up

18 The fierce storm <u>terrified</u> the children. <u>Terrified</u> means—

A entertained

B delighted

C confused

D frightened

19 It was difficult for Alexander to drive through the <u>dense</u> fog. <u>Dense</u> means—

F dirty

G smoky

H thick

J dangerous

20 Mother wanted to paint the <u>dingy</u> room. <u>Dingy</u> means—

A dull

B small

C bright

D damp

Write your answer to the following:

21 The <u>authentic</u> fort had been demolished years earlier. <u>Authentic</u> means—

_____

_____

_____

STOP

Sample A

Which fraction means the same as $\frac{10}{16}$?

A $\frac{1}{8}$ C $\frac{6}{16}$

B $\frac{5}{8}$ D $\frac{2}{3}$

STOP

For questions 1–50, darken the circle for the correct answer, or write in the answer.

1 Which list shows the colleges in order from the earliest date founded?

Year Founded	Name of School
1636	Harvard
1701	Yale
1754	Columbia University
1764	Brown University

A Columbia, Harvard, Brown, Yale

B Harvard, Yale, Columbia, Brown

C Harvard, Yale, Brown, Columbia

D Yale, Brown, Columbia, Harvard

2 The space shuttle *Atlantis* can travel as many as 452,384 miles in one day while in orbit. How would this number be written in words?

F forty-five thousand twenty-three hundred forty-eight

G four hundred fifty-two thousand three hundred eighty-four

H four million fifty-two thousand three hundred eighty-four

J four million five hundred twenty-three thousand eighteen four

3 Which number has a 3 in the tens place?

A 463

B 4,371

C 398

D 830

4 Patti needs $3\frac{1}{2}$ yards of white fabric, $2\frac{1}{3}$ yards of green fabric, $1\frac{1}{2}$ yards of black fabric, and $2\frac{3}{4}$ yards of brown fabric. Choose the list that shows the fabrics from least to greatest amounts.

F white, green, black, brown

G black, green, brown, white

H green, black, white, brown

J brown, black, white, green

5 What fraction of the set of shapes are squares?

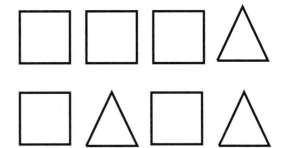

A $\frac{3}{8}$

B $\frac{3}{5}$

C $\frac{5}{8}$

D $\frac{8}{5}$

GO ON

6 If $130 + x = 420$, then $x =$

F   550   H   290

G   390   J   210

7 Which number is in the same fact family as

$3 \times 8 = \square$?

A $\square \times 8 = 16$

B $8 + 3 = \square$

C $6 \times 4 = \square$

D $\square \div 8 = 3$

8 What number is shown here in expanded form?

$5{,}000{,}000 + 500 + 4$

F   50,540

G   550,400

H   5,005,400

J   5,000,504

9 At Wendy's school, the students are selling boxes of candles to raise funds. Wendy has been selling 5 boxes an hour at the mall. Which equation could be used to find x, the number of boxes Wendy sells in 6 hours at this rate?

A $6 \div 5 = x$

B $6 + 5 = x$

C $5x \times 5 = x$

D $6 \times 5 = x$

10 What number would replace the $\square$ to make the number sentence true?

$73 + (68 + 31) = (68 + 31) + \square$

F   99

G   73

H   68

J   31

11 Suzanne's monthly insurance payments will increase by $45 per month. Her current payment is $84. What will her new monthly payment be?

_____

_____

_____

_____

12 There are 13 students in one lunch line and 29 students in another line. How many students would need to move from the second line in order to have the same number of students in both lines?

A   24

B   16

C   8

D   4

13 What is the value of the 9 in 75.09?

F   9 ones

G   9 thousandths

H   9 tenths

J   9 hundredths

14 Which decimal belongs in the box on the number line?

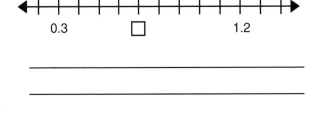

_____

_____

_____

_____

GO ON ➡

15 Wanda is choosing what to wear to school. She has 3 pairs of jeans, 4 tops, and 2 pairs of shoes to choose from. How many different clothing combinations does Wanda have?

A 9

B 12

C 14

D 24

16 If Larry picked one of the cards shown here without looking, which of the cards would he most likely pick?

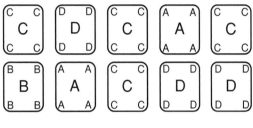

F A

G B

H C

J D

17 It is Carmela's turn in a board game she is playing with her family. What is the probability that Carmela will lose a turn on this spin?

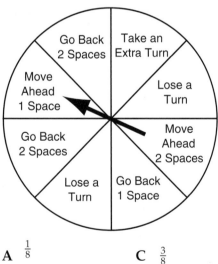

A $\frac{1}{8}$

B $\frac{2}{8}$

C $\frac{3}{8}$

D $\frac{5}{8}$

18 Every morning Sam takes his two dogs, Rocket and Jackpot, for a 35-minute walk. Which equation could be used to find t, the total number of minutes Sam walks his dogs each week?

F $7 + 2 + 35 = t$

G $7 \times 35 = t$

H $7(2 + 35) = t$

J $7 \times \frac{35}{60} = t$

19 Which equation means the same as $9 \times 6 = 54$?

A $54 \times 6 = 9$

B $54 \div 9 = 6$

C $9 \div 6 = 54$

D $54 - 9 = 6$

20 A special machine multiplies any number entered into it by 8. The table shows how the numbers are changed. Which numbers complete the table? Write them in the boxes.

Original number	4	6	9
New number	32		

GO ON➡

21 The table shows Wyatt's earnings over a 5-week period last summer.

Wyatt's Earnings

Week 1	$12
Week 2	$20
Week 3	$15
Week 4	$25
Week 5	$13

Wyatt wanted to earn $40 to buy a remote-controlled car. During which week did he reach his goal?

F week 2

G week 3

H week 4

J week 5

22 The graph shows the population changes in Smithville over the years.

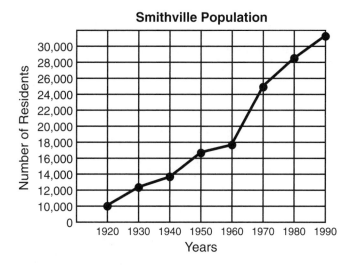

When did Smithville's population grow the most?

A from 1950 to 1960

B from 1960 to 1970

C from 1970 to 1980

D from 1980 to 1990

23 One piece of the puzzle is missing. Which piece is the missing one?

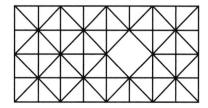

F

G

H

J

24 Jean likes 2 shirts and 3 skirts at a local department store. She can afford to buy only 1 shirt and 1 skirt. How many different combinations are available to Jean?

A 12 **C** 6

B 8 **D** 5

25 How many dots would form the sixth figure if this pattern continues?

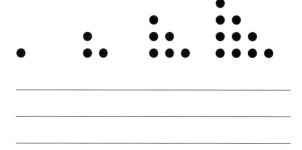

_____

_____

_____

_____

GO ON➡

26 Which tally chart shows the data used in the bar graph?

F		
Cake	卌 卌 卌 卌 卌 卌	
Cookies	卌 卌 |||	
Pie	卌 卌	
Ice Cream	卌 卌 卌 卌 |||	

G		
Cake	卌 卌 卌	
Cookies	卌 卌	
Pie	卌 ||	
Ice Cream	卌 卌 卌	

H		
Cake	卌 卌 卌 卌 卌 卌	
Cookies	卌 卌 卌 卌 卌	
Pie	卌 卌 卌	
Ice Cream	卌 卌 卌 卌 卌 卌 卌	

J		
Cake	卌 卌 卌 卌 卌 卌	
Cookies	卌 卌 卌 卌 ||	
Pie	卌 卌 卌	
Ice Cream	卌 卌 卌 卌 卌 卌 卌	

27 The graph shows the results of a survey taken at the mall.

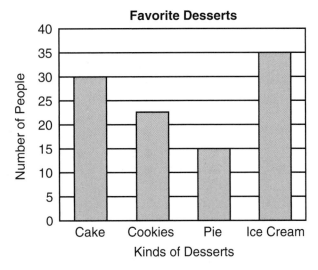

Favorite Desserts

What is the total number of people who liked cake and pie?

A 15   C 45

B 30   D 112

28 The octagons are grouped together in the oval. The other figures are not octagons.

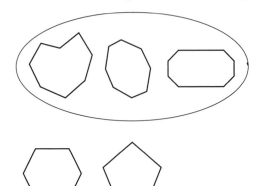

Which shape below is an octagon?

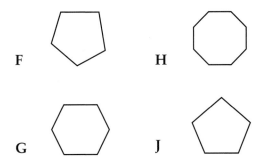

F   H

G   J

29 How many right angles does this figure have?

A 1

B 2

C 4

D none

30 Mick delivered 26, 19, 23, and 20 newspapers on the blocks of his route. What was the average number of newspapers Mick delivered?

_____

_____

_____

_____

GO ON➡

This graph shows the number of videotapes purchased by the public library each month from January through May. Study the graph. Then answer questions 31 and 32.

VIDEOTAPES PURCHASED

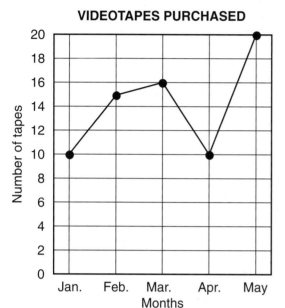

31 How many more tapes were purchased in May than in January?

F 10   H 30

G 20   J 4

32 How many tapes were purchased altogether?

_____

_____

_____

33 The Jordan Middle School held a car wash to raise funds to buy computers. During the first 4 hours, the following number of cars were washed: 46, 59, 64, and 63. What was the average number of cars washed in an hour?

A 64   C 232

B 46   D 58

34 Find the area of a rectangle that is 4 meters by 8 meters.

F 12 square meters   H 36 square meters

G 24 square meters   J 32 square meters

35 Which figure does not show a line of symmetry?

A

C

B

D

36 If the pattern formed by the blocks continues, how many blocks will be needed to make the next shape?

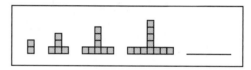

F 12   H 17

G 14   J 20

37 Which transformation moves the figure from position A to position B?

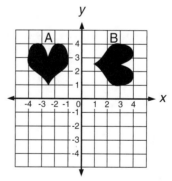

A rotation

B reflection

C translation

D rotation and translation

GO ON➡

38 What is the area of the shaded part of the figure shown here?

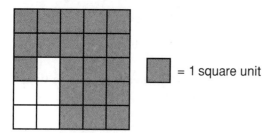

☐ = 1 square unit

F 5 square units

G 11 square units

H 18 square units

J 20 square units

39 Amir drew a picture of the sandbox at his neighborhood playground. What is the perimeter of the sandbox?

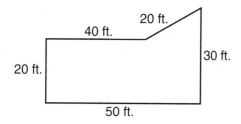

A 100 ft.

B 160 ft.

C 140 ft.

D 80 ft.

40 What is the perimeter of this figure?

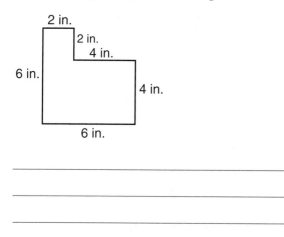

_____

_____

_____

_____

41 Which of the following units of metric measurement is best to use to measure the length of a bike path?

F meter

G kiloliter

H milligram

J kilometer

42 Use your inch ruler and the map to help you answer the question. What is the actual distance from the beach to the airport?

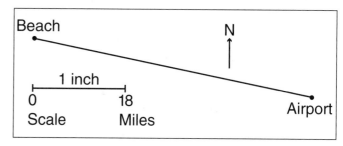

A 36 miles

C 54 miles

B 72 miles

D 62 miles

43 Which best represents the coordinates of the location of 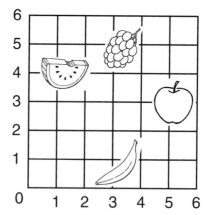 on the map?

F (4, 3)

G (1, 3)

H (1, 4)

J (3, 5)

GO ON➡

44 Yugi was keeping track of how many times each team in his baseball league won a game. The Rangers had more wins than the Tigers. The Bullets had more wins than the Pirates. The Bullets had fewer wins than the Tigers. Which team had the most wins?

_____

_____

_____

45 Which figure is made of all triangles?

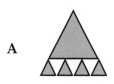

A

C

B

D

46 Barry ordered a ham sandwich for $2.89, a small salad for $1.25, and iced tea for $0.89. What is the *best estimate* of the total cost of his bill?

F $5.00   H $7.00

G $6.00   J $8.00

47 What time will it be in 35 minutes?

A   6:00

B   6:05

C   5:55

D   7:05

48 Maria makes decorative pillows. She can sew a pillow in 25 minutes. What additional information is needed to find out how long it takes Maria to sew an entire set of pillows?

F   the length of each pillow

G   the number of pillows in a set

H   the weight of each pillow

J   the number of sets Maria has made

49 Meili needs to have pieces of fabric that are the same shape and size as the small figure shown here.

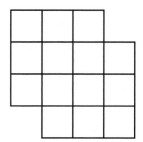

What is the greatest number of these fabric pieces Meili could cut from this large piece of fabric?

A   12

B   14

C   16

D   18

50 The House of Flowers bought 72 flats of seedlings from their wholesaler. There were 96 seedlings per flat. What is the *best estimate* of the number of seedlings that the House of Flowers bought?

F   6,000

G   7,000

H   7,500

J   12,500

STOP

Sample A

$$7\frac{2}{3}$$
$$+10\frac{1}{4}$$

A $17\frac{11}{12}$

B $17\frac{10}{12}$

C $17\frac{3}{7}$

D $18\frac{1}{2}$

E   NH

STOP

For questions 1–14, darken the circle for the correct answer. Darken the circle for NH (Not Here) if the correct answer is not given. If no choices are given, write in your answer.

1   0.17 × 0.05 =

_____

_____

_____

_____

2   878 − 69 =

A   809

B   701

C   398

D   947

E   NH

3   67 × 53 =

F   3,551

G   3,531

H   3,421

J   3,651

K   NH

4

$$\frac{7}{16}$$
$$-\frac{5}{16}$$

A $\frac{3}{4}$

B $\frac{7}{8}$

C $\frac{5}{6}$

D   12

E   NH

5   0.23 × 0.09 =

F   0.0207

G   0.2007

H   0.207

J   0.27

K   NH

6 $\frac{1}{2} \times \frac{1}{8} =$

A $\frac{1}{16}$

B $\frac{1}{6}$

C $\frac{1}{8}$

D $\frac{1}{4}$

E   NH

7 $17\overline{)238}$

F   13 R 7

G   7 R 13

H   13

J   14

K   NH

8

$$\$4.18$$
$$+ \$2.31$$

A $1.87

B $4.39

C $6.49

D $6.59

E   NH

9   The grocery store received a shipment of 120 cases of milk yesterday. If 75 of the cases were whole milk, and the rest were skim milk, then how many of the cases were skim milk?

F   92 cases

G   75 cases

H   60 cases

J   195 cases

K   NH

GO ON ➡

Sample B

Mr. Mendoza uses his own truck at work. If he drove 128 miles last week, and 62 of those miles were for his personal use, how many miles did he drive on the job?

A 190 miles

B 55 miles

C 58 miles

D 66 miles

E NH

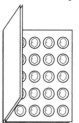 STOP

---

10 Kelly worked $9\frac{1}{3}$ hours at the shoe store last week. She worked $14\frac{1}{3}$ hours this week.

How many more hours did Kelly work this week?

A 5

B $5\frac{1}{3}$

C $5\frac{2}{3}$

D $6\frac{1}{3}$

E NH

11 Leland went to his grandfather's apple orchard to help pick apples. One day he picked 8 baskets of Winesap apples and 13 baskets of Granny Smith apples.

How many baskets of apples did he pick altogether?

F 19 baskets

G 21 baskets

H 23 baskets

J 5 baskets

K NH

---

12 Mr. Ralston has 420 coins in his collection. Of those coins, 70% are very valuable.

How many of the coins are very valuable?

A 168

B 210

C 252

D 294

E NH

13 The diameter of the sun measures 1,392,000 kilometers.

What is that number rounded to the nearest hundred thousand miles?

F 1,300,000

G 1,390,000

H 1,395,000

J 1,400,000

K NH

14 Ms. Nakamura's class has only 1 computer. She lets each student use it for 10 minutes at a time.

How many students can use the computer during the 60 minutes before school?

_____

_____

_____

_____

STOP

Hawaii

The students in Rachel's class are preparing travel guides for places that they have visited. Rachel wants to do a travel guide about Hawaii, where she went on vacation with her family. She wants to let others know what Hawaii is like. She wants to inform everyone about the great places she visited in Hawaii.

Sample A

What would Rachel **not** want to include in her travel guide?

A   the names of beaches she visited

B   a description of Hawaii's climate

C   the names of the counties in Hawaii

D   the names of national parks in Hawaii

 STOP

For questions 1–5, darken the circle for the correct answer.

1   Rachel wants to know the meaning of the word *dormant*. Where should she look?

    A   a dictionary   C   an atlas

    B   a thesaurus   D   a history book

2   Rachel wants to read some travel brochures about Hawaii. To find the nearest travel bureau, she should look in—

    F   a dictionary.

    G   a thesaurus.

    H   an atlas.

    J   a telephone directory.

3   Rachel has found a book called *The Hawaiian Islands*. She wants information about the climate of Hawaii. What part of the book would help her find her topic quickly?

    A   the copyright page

    B   the introduction

    C   the index

    D   the title page

4   Which guide words might mark the page on which Rachel would find the word *volcanic*?

    F   void–volume   H   volunteer–vote

    G   vivid–voice   J   visual–vitamin

5   In which part of *The Hawaiian Islands* would Rachel find the author's name?

    _____

    _____

    _____

GO ON ➡

Here are the Table of Contents and Index from *The Hawaiian Islands,* the book Rachel found in the library. Study them carefully. Then answer questions 6–11.

Table of Contents

Index

6   Which chapter should Rachel read to learn about the lakes and rivers in Hawaii?

A   Chapter 1

B   Chapter 2

C   Chapter 3

D   Chapter 4

7   Which pages would have information about where active volcanoes are found in Hawaii?

F   6–7

G   9–11

H   15–16

J   37–38

8   Which pages would have information about the Polynesians, the first Hawaiians?

A   6–7

B   15–16

C   35–36

D   56–57

9   Chapter 4 contains information on all of these except—

F   national parks to visit.

G   the best places for surfing.

H   the government of Hawaii.

J   harbor towns along the coasts.

10   Which chapter should Rachel read to find out about the way the land in Hawaii was formed?

_____

_____

_____

_____

11   Which pages would have information about the daily temperatures in Hawaii?

A   6–7

B   9–11

C   12–13

D   37–38

GO ON➡

Here is a rough draft of the first part of Rachel's travel guide. Read the rough draft carefully. Then answer questions 12–19.

Hawaii

Do you want to have the greatest time in the world? If you do, and
(1)   (2)

you do then Hawaii is the vacation spot for you.

Hawaii is one of the 50 states of the United States. It is the only
(3)   (4)

state that is not part of the mainland of North America. Hawaii is our
(5)

southernmost state.

Hawaii has many beautiful and interesting sights to see. The
(6)   (7)

islands are a wonderful place to experience volcanoes. You can
(8)

experience magnificent waterfalls and beautiful beaches. The weather
(9)

is warm year–round, so every day is a good day for any outdoor plans.

The people of Hawaii have many colorful customs. You can enjoy
(10)   (11)

interesting food and music. You can also watch folk dancing, parades, and
(12)

special events. You can travel from island to island. By boat or by plane.
(13)   (14)

---

12 Which sentence does <u>not</u> belong in Rachel's travel guide? Write the number.

_____

_____

_____

_____

13 What is the best way to write sentence 2?

F   If you do, then Hawaii is the vacation spot for you.

G   If you do, then you do know that Hawaii is the vacation spot for you.

H   If you do want to, then you do want to have Hawaii as a vacation spot for you.

J   If you want to, then you want to visit Hawaii for vacation.

GO ON ➡

14 Which of the following sentences best combines sentences 4 and 5 without changing their meaning?

A Hawaii is the only state that is not part of the mainland of North America, and is our southernmost state.

B Hawaii is our southernmost state and Hawaii is the only state that is not part of the mainland of North America.

C It is the only state that is not part of the mainland of North America, and is our southernmost state.

D Hawaii is our southernmost state, and the only state that is not part of the mainland of North America.

15 Which of the following sentences best combines sentences 7 and 8 without changing their meaning?

F The islands are a wonderful place to experience volcanoes and a wonderful place to experience magnificent waterfalls and beaches.

G The islands are a wonderful place to experience volcanoes and to experience magnificent waterfalls and beautiful beaches.

H Volcanoes, waterfalls, and beautiful beaches in the islands are wonderful places to experience.

J The islands are a wonderful place to experience volcanoes, magnificent waterfalls, and beautiful beaches.

16 Which of these sentences could be added before sentence 9?

A Hawaii has several active volcanoes.

B Hawaii has a very pleasant climate.

C The original natives of Hawaii were Polynesians.

D Hawaii has eight major islands.

17 What supporting information could be added after sentence 11?

F For example, poi is a favorite native Hawaiian delicacy made from cooked, fermented taro root.

G There are many things to do in Hawaii.

H Hawaii is in the Pacific Ocean.

J There are other interesting vacation spots.

18 What is the most colorful way to write sentence 11?

A You can enjoy some food and some music.

B You can eat food and listen to music.

C You can enjoy native Hawaiian food and music.

D As it is written.

19 Which group of words in Rachel's travel guide is <u>not</u> a complete sentence? Write the number of the group of words.

_____

_____

_____

_____

GO ON

Here is the next part of Rachel's rough draft for her travel guide. This part has certain words and phrases underlined. Read the draft carefully. Then answer questions 20–29.

Hawaii is made up of eight major islands. The state capital,
(15)   (16)

Honolulu, is located at the island of Oahu. All the islands was formed by
(17)

volcanoes. Today these volcanoes are the islands mountains. Mauna Loa
(18)   (19)

and Kilauea are Hawaiis' only active volcanoes.

Hawaii has more than 1,000 miles of coastline. Much of the coastline
(20)   (21)

is covered with white sand beaches. Some of the coastline is covered with
(22)

black sand sand made from lava. On the island of Kauai, there is a beach
(23)

called "Barking Sands." When walked upon in dry weather, the sand
(24)

makes a crunching noise that sounds like dogs barking.

Hawaii has mildest temperatures all year. The cool ocean breezes
(25)   (26)

help created a wonderful climate. For this reason people sometimes call
(27)

Hawaii "Paradise."

---

20 In sentence 16, <u>is located at the island of Oahu</u> is best written—

F   is located upon the island of Oahu

G   is located in the island of Oahu

H   is located on the island of Oahu

J   As it is written.

21 In sentence 17, <u>All the islands was formed</u> is best written—

A   All the island is formed

B   All the islands is forming

C   All the islands were formed

D   As it is written.

GO ON➡

22 In sentence 18, <u>volcanoes are the islands mountains</u> is best written—

F volcanoes are the islands' mountains

G volcano's are the islands mountains

H volcanoes are the island's mountains

J As it is written.

23 In sentence 19, <u>Hawaiis' only active volcanoes</u> is best written—

A Hawaiis only active volcanoes

B Hawaii's only active volcanoes

C Hawaiis' only, active volcanoes

D As it is written.

24 In sentence 21, <u>is covered</u> is best written—

F will be covered

G was covered

H were covered

J As it is written.

25 In sentence 22, <u>black sand sand made</u> is best written—

A black, sand sand made

B black sand, sand made

C black sand made

D As it is written.

26 In sentence 23, <u>a beach</u> is best written—

F the beach

G an beach

H the beaches

J As it is written.

27 In sentence 25, <u>has mildest temperatures</u> is best written—

A has mild temperatures

B has most mild temperatures

C has milder temperatures

D As it is written.

28 In sentence 26, <u>breezes help created</u> is best written—

F breezes help creates

G breezes help create

H breezes help creating

J As it is written.

29 In sentence 27, <u>For this reason people</u> is best written—

A For this, reason people

B For, this reason people

C For this reason, people

D As it is written.

GO ON➡

For questions 30–41, read each sentence carefully. If one of the words is misspelled, darken the circle for that word. If all of the words are spelled correctly, then darken the circle for *No mistake*.

30   He was positive his homework was corect. No mistake
              F   G   H   J

31   The wooden shingel fell off the roof during the thunderstorm. No mistake
              A   B   C   D

32   Teofila injered herself when she fell at the skating rink. No mistake
              F   G   H   J

33   Miriam had a wonderfull time at the party. No mistake
                        A   B   C   D

34   The freighter crossed the Pacific Ocean in two weeks. No mistake
              F   G   H   J

35   Edward shoped around to get the best price on a new stereo. No mistake
                    A   B   C   D

36   The collie wagged its tale as it approached us. No mistake
              F   G   H   J

37   His automobile accident was caused by a leak in the break line. No mistake
                              A   B   C   D

38   The new golf coarse is located west of town. No mistake
                          F   G   H   J

39   The view from the mountain was spectaculer. No mistake
              A   B   C   D

40   Sam complimented Lynn on her rousing speech. No mistake
                    F   G   H   J

41   Every year Hector donates money to several charitys. No mistake
                                A   B   C   D

STOP

124

UNIT 2:
SIX READING SKILLS

pp. 12–15 **1.** B **2.** The balloon will get smaller since the air escapes when it deflates. **3.** J **4.** B **5.** G **6.** C **7.** The fuel reservoir holds gasoline. It is the tank. **8.** H **9.** B **10.** An epidemic is when many people, animals, or plants get sick. **11.** H **12.** A **13.** F **14.** to travel

pp. 16–19 **1.** B **2.** H **3.** C **4.** The Arctic ice rests on the ocean. **5.** H **6.** C **7.** They are in greatest danger right after the baby's birth. **8.** F **9.** B **10.** J **11.** Peggy should inspect engine 5 first, after she signs in. **12.** C **13.** H **14.** B **15.** The story takes place in southwestern Colorado.

pp. 20–23 **1.** A **2.** G **3.** The story is mostly about how Bartholdi got his idea from a girl he once saw. **4.** A **5.** H **6.** A **7.** The main idea is that Martin did not realize how hard it is to take care of a dog. **8.** H **9.** B **10.** This story is mostly about the four types of poisonous snakes found in the United States. **11.** F **12.** B **13.** This passage is mostly about how Levi Strauss invented the first pair of blue jeans.

pp. 24–27 **1.** Missy rubbed her eyes because she was trying to wake up. **2.** C **3.** G **4.** D **5.** F **6.** She was excited because she looked forward to growing her own vegetables. **7.** B **8.** She will be pleasantly surprised. **9.** He will probably write a thank-you note to his aunt. **10.** J

pp. 28–33 **1.** D **2.** There were 27.8 million cars. **3.** It is about 6 billion. **4.** G **5.** C **6.** J **7.** D **8.** J **9.** B **10.** Inventions that did not make money. **11.** F **12.** Alur felt angry. **13.** B **14.** It was performed to bring happiness and a feeling of connection with those who died.

pp. 34–35 **1.** B **2.** F **3.** D **4.** F **5.** D

UNIT 3:
READING COMPREHENSION

pp. 36–43 **SA.** B **1.** B **2.** A sphinx is an imaginary animal with a human head and the body of a lion. **3.** H **4.** C **5.** F **6.** A **7.** H **8.** D **9.** G **10.** He arrived at the hospital in time. **11.** stranded **12.** A **13.** F **14.** C **15.** G **16.** after they came to Europe or before they came to America **17.** D **18.** G **19.** B **20.** H **21.** the Chinese **22.** D **23.** F **24.** B **25.** H **26.** D **27.** H **28.** C **29.** G **30.** Slip the rubber band through to the middle of the paper. **31.** A

pp. 44–51 **SA.** D **1.** C **2.** J **3.** to raise money to buy bats and balls **4.** B **5.** To take a job, as her family needed money following her father's death. **6.** G **7.** A **8.** J **9.** B **10.** J **11.** C **12.** chicken **13.** H **14.** C **15.** H **16.** C **17.** J **18.** B **19.** G **20.** D **21.** G **22.** A **23.** H **24.** They hoped to become rich quickly. **25.** B **26.** G **27.** A **28.** to tell the history of the California Gold Rush **29.** The weather was threatening. **30.** H **31.** B **32.** G

UNIT 4:
READING VOCABULARY

p. 52 **SA.** D **1.** D **2.** J **3.** B **4.** G **5.** B **6.** H **7.** B **8.** cold

p. 53 **SA.** A **1.** C **2.** G **3.** C **4.** H

p. 54 **SA.** A **1.** A **2.** J **3.** C **4.** difficult **5.** F **6.** A

pp. 55–57 **SA.** D **1.** C **2.** J **3.** A **4.** F **5.** B **6.** J **7.** C **8.** F **9.** tired **SB.** C **10.** A **11.** J **12.** C **13.** F **14.** D **SC.** A **15.** H **16.** D **17.** F **18.** C **19.** J **20.** C **21.** G **22.** the story

UNIT 5:
MATH PROBLEM-SOLVING PLAN

p. 59 **Step 1.** to draw a map illustrating Mr. Gonzalez's trip **Step 2.** He drove 45 miles to Boston from Manorville. From Boston he drove 15 miles north to Oaktown. Manorville is west of Boston. **Step 3.** Draw a map and label it. **Step 5.** Yes, because the diagram drawn shows the information included in the problem.

p. 60 **Step 1.** Is $19.50 the approximated cost for 5 books? If not, indicate what error Su Ling may have made. **Step 2.** Each book costs $4.95. Su Ling bought 5 books. Su Link estimated the total cost to be $19.50. **Step 3.** Calculate: Multiply $4.95 x 5 **Step 4.** $4.95 x 5 = $24.75. Su Ling's estimate of $19.50 was wrong. Her mistake may have been that she rounded off $4.95 to be $4.00. Then she estimated the total cost to be just under $20 instead of just under $25. **Step 5.** Yes, because Su Ling did estimate incorrectly and the explanation offered is one possible explanation.

UNIT 6:
MATH PROBLEM SOLVING

p. 61 **SA.** A **1.** 12.09, 12.2, 12.25, 12.53 **2.** C **3.** J **4.** D **5.** H

p. 62 **SA.** D **1.** C **2.** F **3.** A **4.** H **5.** 7 **6.** B

p. 63 **SA.** B **1.** D **2.** G **3.** B **4.** F **5.** C **6.** 11

pp. 64–65 **SA.** B **1.** C **2.** J **3.** $24.75 **4.** C **5.** G **6.** C **7.** F **8.** 123 **9.** A **10.** H

p. 66 **SA.** D **1.** C **2.** 240 **3.** G

p. 67 **SA.** D **1.** C **2.** 8,000 **3.** G **4.** D

pp. 68–69 **SA.** B **1.** bike rack, tables, water **2.** D **3.** 55 m **4.** G **5.** C **6.** F **7.** C **8.** G **9.** D **10.** F **11.** B

pp. 70–71 **SA.** C **1.** D **2.** 12:15 **3.** F **4.** C **5.** F **6.** D **7.** F **8.** C **9.** G **10.** C. **11.** 2 cm

p. 72 **SA.** A **1.** 125 **2.** B **3.** F **4.** D

p. 73 **SA.** D **1.** D **2.** F **3.** C **4.** H **5.** A **6.** 12 R4 **7.** K **8.** D

p. 74 **SA.** D **1.** B **2.** H **3.** C **4.** $2,056

pp. 75–76 **SA.** B **SB.** K **1.** E **2.** G **3.** B **4.** K **5.** C **6.** G **7.** B **8.** G **9.** 5,950 **10.** A **11.** K **12.** A **13.** H **14.** B **15.** G

pp. 77–83 **SA.** D **1.** A **2.** J **3.** C **4.** J **5.** C **6.** J **7.** B **8.** 3 hundredths **9.** H **10.** A **11.** H **12.** D **13.** G **14.** B **15.** H **16.** 24 **17.** C **18.** F **19.** C **20.** H **21.** A **22.** H **23.** 45 **24.** A **25.** G **26.** C **27.** G **28.** 21 **29.** B **30.** H **31.** C **32.** G **33.** C **34.** G **35.** 48 ft. **36.** A **37.** H **38.** D **39.** H **40.** D **41.** 2 **42.** F **43.** A **44.** H **45.** C **46.** on the 7th **47.** J **48.** B **49.** J **50.** B

UNIT 7:
LANGUAGE

pp. 84–89 **SA.** B **1.** B **2.** Chapter 6 **3.** G **4.** D **5.** J **6.** D **7.** G **8.** C **9.** H **10.** B **11.** G **12.** C **13.** F **14.** 6 **15.** A **16.** G **17.** C **18.** G **19.** A **20.** H **21.** D **22.** G

p. 90 **SA.** A **1.** D **2.** J **3.** C **4.** F **5.** B **6.** G **7.** A **8.** F

pp. 91–95 **SA.** C **1.** A **2.** G **3.** B **4.** Sentence 6 **5.** J **6.** B **7.** J **8.** C **9.** H **10.** A **11.** G **12.** C **13.** J **14.** A **15.** J **16.** D **17.** G **18.** B **19.** H **20.** D **21.** G **22.** A **23.** F **24.** B **25.** J **26.** B **27.** H **28.** B

UNIT 8:
PRACTICE TEST 1:
READING COMPREHENSION

pp. 96–104 **SA.** D **1.** B **2.** to fish for bass **3.** G **4.** the sunset, the animal sounds, and the snapping turtle **5.** D **6.** H **7.** A **8.** clams and oyster shells **9.** H **10.** D **11.** F **12.** B **13.** J **14.** She boils them in water for five to ten minutes. **15.** B **16.** F **17.** extremely important **18.** C **19.** F **20.** D **21.** F **22.** D **23.** F **24.** B **25.** J **26.** A **27.** G **28.** C **29.** H **30.** There were very few trees growing on the Great Plains. **31.** C **32.** H **33.** B **34.** H **35.** Saturday and Sunday, April 20 and 21 **36.** B **37.** Grandma's car had been ruined in the flood. **38.** G **39.** C **40.** J

UNIT 9:
PRACTICE TEST 2:
READING VOCABULARY

pp. 105–107 **SA.** A **1.** D **2.** G **3.** C **4.** H **5.** B **6.** G **7.** A **8.** F **9.** ridiculous **SB.** B **10.** D **11.** F **12.** C **13.** J **14.** C **SC.** D **15.** F **16.** C **17.** H **18.** D **19.** H **20.** A **21.** real

UNIT 10:
PRACTICE TEST 3
PART 1:
MATH PROBLEM SOLVING

pp. 108–115 **SA.** B **1.** B **2.** G **3.** D **4.** G **5.** C **6.** H **7.** D **8.** J **9.** D **10.** G **11.** $129 **12.** C **13.** J **14.** 0.7 **15.** D **16.** H **17.** B **18.** G **19.** B **20.** 48 and 72 **21.** G **22.** B **23.** J **24.** C **25.** 21 **26.** J **27.** C **28.** H **29.** D **30.** 22 **31.** F **32.** 71 **33.** D **34.** J **35.** B **36.** G **37.** A **38.** J **39.** B **40.** 24 in. **41.** J **42.** C **43.** H **44.** The Rangers had the most wins. **45.** A **46.** F **47.** B **48.** G **49.** B **50.** G

PART 2:
MATH PROCEDURES

pp. 116–117 **SA.** A **1.** 0.0085 **2.** A **3.** F **4.** E **5.** F **6.** A **7.** J **8.** C **9.** K **SB.** D **10.** A **11.** G **12.** D **13.** J **14.** 6

UNIT 11:
PRACTICE TEST 4:
LANGUAGE

pp. 118–124 **SA.** C **1.** A **2.** J **3.** C **4.** F **5.** the title page **6.** A **7.** F **8.** B **9.** H **10.** Chapter 1 **11.** B **12.** 3 **13.** F **14.** D **15.** J **16.** B **17.** F **18.** C **19.** 14 **20.** H **21.** C **22.** F **23.** B **24.** J **25.** C **26.** J **27.** A **28.** G **29.** C **30.** H **31.** B **32.** F **33.** A **34.** J **35.** A **36.** H **37.** C **38.** F **39.** C **40.** J **41.** C

Answer Sheet

STUDENT'S NAME		SCHOOL:

LAST   **FIRST**   **MI**

TEACHER:

FEMALE ○   MALE ○

BIRTH DATE

MONTH	DAY		YEAR	
Jan ○	⓪	⓪	⓪	⓪
Feb ○	①	①	①	①
Mar ○	②	②	②	②
Apr ○	③	③	③	③
May ○		④	④	④
Jun ○		⑤	⑤	⑤
Jul ○		⑥	⑥	⑥
Aug ○		⑦	⑦	⑦
Sep ○		⑧	⑧	⑧
Oct ○		⑨	⑨	⑨
Nov ○				
Dec ○				

GRADE ④ ⑤ ⑥ ⑦ ⑧

(Name grid columns with bubbles ○ and letters A–Z for each column)

Fill in the circle for each multiple-choice answer. Write the answers to the open-ended questions on a separate sheet of paper.

TEST 1   Reading Comprehension

SA Ⓐ Ⓑ Ⓒ Ⓓ
1 Ⓐ Ⓑ Ⓒ Ⓓ
2 OPEN ENDED
3 Ⓕ Ⓖ Ⓗ Ⓙ
4 OPEN ENDED
5 Ⓐ Ⓑ Ⓒ Ⓓ
6 Ⓕ Ⓖ Ⓗ Ⓙ

7 Ⓐ Ⓑ Ⓒ Ⓓ
8 OPEN ENDED
9 Ⓕ Ⓖ Ⓗ Ⓙ
10 Ⓐ Ⓑ Ⓒ Ⓓ
11 Ⓕ Ⓖ Ⓗ Ⓙ
12 Ⓐ Ⓑ Ⓒ Ⓓ
13 Ⓕ Ⓖ Ⓗ Ⓙ

14 OPEN ENDED
15 Ⓐ Ⓑ Ⓒ Ⓓ
16 Ⓕ Ⓖ Ⓗ Ⓙ
17 OPEN ENDED
18 Ⓐ Ⓑ Ⓒ Ⓓ
19 Ⓕ Ⓖ Ⓗ Ⓙ
20 Ⓐ Ⓑ Ⓒ Ⓓ

21 Ⓕ Ⓖ Ⓗ Ⓙ
22 Ⓐ Ⓑ Ⓒ Ⓓ
23 Ⓕ Ⓖ Ⓗ Ⓙ
24 Ⓐ Ⓑ Ⓒ Ⓓ
25 Ⓕ Ⓖ Ⓗ Ⓙ
26 Ⓐ Ⓑ Ⓒ Ⓓ
27 Ⓕ Ⓖ Ⓗ Ⓙ

28 Ⓐ Ⓑ Ⓒ Ⓓ
29 Ⓕ Ⓖ Ⓗ Ⓙ
30 OPEN ENDED
31 Ⓐ Ⓑ Ⓒ Ⓓ
32 Ⓕ Ⓖ Ⓗ Ⓙ
33 Ⓐ Ⓑ Ⓒ Ⓓ
34 Ⓕ Ⓖ Ⓗ Ⓙ

35 OPEN ENDED
36 Ⓐ Ⓑ Ⓒ Ⓓ
37 OPEN ENDED
38 Ⓕ Ⓖ Ⓗ Ⓙ
39 Ⓐ Ⓑ Ⓒ Ⓓ
40 Ⓕ Ⓖ Ⓗ Ⓙ

TEST 2   Reading Vocabulary

SA Ⓐ Ⓑ Ⓒ Ⓓ
1 Ⓐ Ⓑ Ⓒ Ⓓ
2 Ⓕ Ⓖ Ⓗ Ⓙ
3 Ⓐ Ⓑ Ⓒ Ⓓ

4 Ⓕ Ⓖ Ⓗ Ⓙ
5 Ⓐ Ⓑ Ⓒ Ⓓ
6 Ⓕ Ⓖ Ⓗ Ⓙ
7 Ⓐ Ⓑ Ⓒ Ⓓ

8 Ⓕ Ⓖ Ⓗ Ⓙ
9 OPEN ENDED
10 Ⓐ Ⓑ Ⓒ Ⓓ
SB Ⓐ Ⓑ Ⓒ Ⓓ

11 Ⓕ Ⓖ Ⓗ Ⓙ
12 Ⓐ Ⓑ Ⓒ Ⓓ
13 Ⓐ Ⓑ Ⓒ Ⓓ
14 Ⓐ Ⓑ Ⓒ Ⓓ

SC Ⓐ Ⓑ Ⓒ Ⓓ
15 Ⓕ Ⓖ Ⓗ Ⓙ
16 Ⓐ Ⓑ Ⓒ Ⓓ
17 Ⓕ Ⓖ Ⓗ Ⓙ

18 Ⓐ Ⓑ Ⓒ Ⓓ
19 Ⓕ Ⓖ Ⓗ Ⓙ
20 Ⓐ Ⓑ Ⓒ Ⓓ
21 OPEN ENDED

Part 1: Math Problem Solving

(D)	9 Ⓐ Ⓑ Ⓒ Ⓓ	18 Ⓕ Ⓖ Ⓗ Ⓙ	27 Ⓐ Ⓑ Ⓒ Ⓓ	36 Ⓕ Ⓖ Ⓗ Ⓙ	45 Ⓐ Ⓑ Ⓒ Ⓓ
Ⓑ Ⓒ Ⓓ	10 Ⓕ Ⓖ Ⓗ Ⓙ	19 Ⓐ Ⓑ Ⓒ Ⓓ	28 Ⓕ Ⓖ Ⓗ Ⓙ	37 Ⓐ Ⓑ Ⓒ Ⓓ	46 Ⓕ Ⓖ Ⓗ Ⓙ
Ⓕ Ⓖ Ⓗ Ⓙ	11 OPEN ENDED	20 OPEN ENDED	29 Ⓐ Ⓑ Ⓒ Ⓓ	38 Ⓕ Ⓖ Ⓗ Ⓙ	47 Ⓐ Ⓑ Ⓒ Ⓓ
3 Ⓐ Ⓑ Ⓒ Ⓓ	12 Ⓐ Ⓑ Ⓒ Ⓓ	21 Ⓕ Ⓖ Ⓗ Ⓙ	30 OPEN ENDED	39 Ⓐ Ⓑ Ⓒ Ⓓ	48 Ⓕ Ⓖ Ⓗ Ⓙ
4 Ⓕ Ⓖ Ⓗ Ⓙ	13 Ⓕ Ⓖ Ⓗ Ⓙ	22 Ⓐ Ⓑ Ⓒ Ⓓ	31 Ⓕ Ⓖ Ⓗ Ⓙ	40 OPEN ENDED	49 Ⓐ Ⓑ Ⓒ Ⓓ
5 Ⓐ Ⓑ Ⓒ Ⓓ	14 OPEN ENDED	23 Ⓕ Ⓖ Ⓗ Ⓙ	32 OPEN ENDED	41 Ⓕ Ⓖ Ⓗ Ⓙ	50 Ⓕ Ⓖ Ⓗ Ⓙ
6 Ⓕ Ⓖ Ⓗ Ⓙ	15 Ⓐ Ⓑ Ⓒ Ⓓ	24 Ⓐ Ⓑ Ⓒ Ⓓ	33 Ⓐ Ⓑ Ⓒ Ⓓ	42 Ⓐ Ⓑ Ⓒ Ⓓ	
7 Ⓐ Ⓑ Ⓒ Ⓓ	16 Ⓕ Ⓖ Ⓗ Ⓙ	25 OPEN ENDED	34 Ⓕ Ⓖ Ⓗ Ⓙ	43 Ⓕ Ⓖ Ⓗ Ⓙ	
8 Ⓕ Ⓖ Ⓗ Ⓙ	17 Ⓐ Ⓑ Ⓒ Ⓓ	26 Ⓕ Ⓖ Ⓗ Ⓙ	35 Ⓐ Ⓑ Ⓒ Ⓓ	44 OPEN ENDED	

Part 2: Math Procedures

SA Ⓐ Ⓑ Ⓒ Ⓓ Ⓔ	3 Ⓕ Ⓖ Ⓗ Ⓙ Ⓚ	6 Ⓐ Ⓑ Ⓒ Ⓓ Ⓔ	9 Ⓕ Ⓖ Ⓗ Ⓙ Ⓚ	11 Ⓕ Ⓖ Ⓗ Ⓙ Ⓚ	14 OPEN ENDED
1 OPEN ENDED	4 Ⓐ Ⓑ Ⓒ Ⓓ Ⓔ	7 Ⓕ Ⓖ Ⓗ Ⓙ Ⓚ	SB Ⓐ Ⓑ Ⓒ Ⓓ Ⓔ	12 Ⓐ Ⓑ Ⓒ Ⓓ Ⓔ	
2 Ⓐ Ⓑ Ⓒ Ⓓ Ⓔ	5 Ⓕ Ⓖ Ⓗ Ⓙ Ⓚ	8 Ⓐ Ⓑ Ⓒ Ⓓ Ⓔ	10 Ⓐ Ⓑ Ⓒ Ⓓ Ⓔ	13 Ⓕ Ⓖ Ⓗ Ⓙ Ⓚ	

TEST 4   Language

SA Ⓐ Ⓑ Ⓒ Ⓓ	7 Ⓕ Ⓖ Ⓗ Ⓙ	14 Ⓐ Ⓑ Ⓒ Ⓓ	21 Ⓐ Ⓑ Ⓒ Ⓓ	28 Ⓕ Ⓖ Ⓗ Ⓙ	35 Ⓐ Ⓑ Ⓒ Ⓓ
1 Ⓐ Ⓑ Ⓒ Ⓓ	8 Ⓐ Ⓑ Ⓒ Ⓓ	15 Ⓕ Ⓖ Ⓗ Ⓙ	22 Ⓕ Ⓖ Ⓗ Ⓙ	29 Ⓐ Ⓑ Ⓒ Ⓓ	36 Ⓕ Ⓖ Ⓗ Ⓙ
2 Ⓕ Ⓖ Ⓗ Ⓙ	9 Ⓕ Ⓖ Ⓗ Ⓙ	16 Ⓐ Ⓑ Ⓒ Ⓓ	23 Ⓐ Ⓑ Ⓒ Ⓓ	30 Ⓕ Ⓖ Ⓗ Ⓙ	37 Ⓐ Ⓑ Ⓒ Ⓓ
3 Ⓐ Ⓑ Ⓒ Ⓓ	10 OPEN ENDED	17 Ⓕ Ⓖ Ⓗ Ⓙ	24 Ⓕ Ⓖ Ⓗ Ⓙ	31 Ⓐ Ⓑ Ⓒ Ⓓ	38 Ⓕ Ⓖ Ⓗ Ⓙ
4 Ⓕ Ⓖ Ⓗ Ⓙ	11 Ⓐ Ⓑ Ⓒ Ⓓ	18 Ⓐ Ⓑ Ⓒ Ⓓ	25 Ⓐ Ⓑ Ⓒ Ⓓ	32 Ⓕ Ⓖ Ⓗ Ⓙ	39 Ⓐ Ⓑ Ⓒ Ⓓ
5 OPEN ENDED	12 OPEN ENDED	19 OPEN ENDED	26 Ⓕ Ⓖ Ⓗ Ⓙ	33 Ⓐ Ⓑ Ⓒ Ⓓ	40 Ⓕ Ⓖ Ⓗ Ⓙ
6 Ⓐ Ⓑ Ⓒ Ⓓ	13 Ⓕ Ⓖ Ⓗ Ⓙ	20 Ⓕ Ⓖ Ⓗ Ⓙ	27 Ⓐ Ⓑ Ⓒ Ⓓ	34 Ⓕ Ⓖ Ⓗ Ⓙ	41 Ⓐ Ⓑ Ⓒ Ⓓ